STEAK

FROM FIELD TO TABLE

by MARCUS POLMAN

BETTERWAY HOME

CINCINNATI, OHIO

WWW.BETTERWAYBOOKS.COM

From field to table

This book is meant for people who appreciate a good piece of steak that is generously fried in butter, bloody red and lukewarm on the inside with a crispy crust. So tender that you can cut it with a fork. With crispy golden fries (do not forget the crackling fleur de sel), topped with a sumptuous full-fat, crisp, home-made Béarnaise sauce. A meal fit for a king and I cannot help but imagine that even the most inveterate vegetarians would have a hard time resisting this.

This book is very informative and it contains some very useful advice. We do not try to help you to dress up tough meat from old dairy cows that is sold as steak, but rather show you how to prepare quality meat from prime animals that date back several generations (such as Aberdeen Angus cattle that I encountered in Scotland). These are free range animals that led a good life without any stress and that grazed on natural food such as grass, clover, buttercups, herbs... That works.

In short: this is a recipe book and reading book about real meat for real connoisseurs. Meat that is given sufficient time to ripen 'to the bone', as butchers say. Meat that is a delight to put into your mouth. This is good meat for 'meatarians' such as myself because when I eat meat I do not compromise as I enjoy the best.

As you may have noticed the classic steak is busy making a comeback, as are brasseries and bistros, but often in a hipper version: an interior with white tiles, to contrast with black and white lounge benches. Some of them even feature a retro version with an unmistakable French touch. Classic items such as steak and French fries are very prominent on their menus. But also a chic côté de boeuf, with denomination of origin, which is wheeled to the table on a trolley to be sliced at the table. Increasingly brisket and porterhouse are also making their way onto menus. Butchers are a part of the process as they sell dry-aged Aberdeen Angus ribeye with a label that shows the name of

the organic family farm where the meat came from. This does not only include the usual suspects such as ox fillet and sirloin, since less common cuts (thick skirt, peeled escalope) are also making their way into butcheries.

These cuts of meat may cost more than others, but a true meatarian understands that it is better to eat high quality meat less frequently than to eat a piece of meat everyday that pushes the boundaries of the definition of the word. If you can afford to spend a little bit more, try to buy local organic beef or Creekstone Farm Prime USDA corn-fed Angus steak from your local butcher (or if you prefer, directly from a farm stall that you pass on a Saturday morning), then make sure that you do not mess up the preparation of such a prime piece of meat. To this end, *Steak: From Field to Table* is an essential tool. This book contains knowledge I have gained myself based on numerous interviews with butchers, slaughterers, breeders, farmers, chefs and culinary experts during my quest for the perfect steak. From Amsterdam to Brandwijk. From New York to Paris.

But of course ... The Perfect Steak does not exist. I therefore decided to ask culinary connoisseurs, including butcher trainers and restaurant critics, to tell me what they thought was a perfect steak, including their own secret tips.

AFTER READING THIS BOOK, YOU WILL NEVER COOK A STEAK ANY OTHER WAY.

I wish you much carnivorous pleasure.

Marcus Polman

*P.S.
A vegan also assisted me: Lisette – *Veggie in Pumps* – Kreischer, the nicest vegan in the Netherlands. Tips are given to anyone who would rather sink their teeth into a contemporary seitan steak (see page 157).

5

STEAK

FROM FIELD TO TABLE

Table of contents

STEAK

FROM FIELD TO TABLE

Beef Basics

How to fry the perfect steak

Pan

The ideal pan is made of steel with a thick bottom. It is resistant to high temperatures, with optimum heat distribution. Note the correct size (2 steaks: 9 ½ inches in diameter).

Meat

Do not simply buy a piece of meat from a butcher. Stick with the best organic quality. Ask questions and be exact. For example: do not ask for steak, but a steak from the flank (nice and tender). Rather ask for a freshly cut rib-eye or sirloin, marbled with intramuscular fat. You can decide to buy fresh or matured (on the bone) meat. And what about breed and age?

Butter

Creamy butter, unsalted.

Salt

Coarse salt sea from the grinder for an extra crispy effect. For example: a subtle fleur de sel or a mild, flaky Maldon salt.

Pepper

Black pepper. Fresh and coarsely ground, or crushed.

Foil

Let your steak rest for at least 5 minutes, loosely wrapped in a 'tunnel' of aluminum foil, on a grille with a plate for collecting liquids below.

Sauce

A tangy classic such as a Béarnaise sauce. Smooth and served lukewarm.

Knife

Sharp knife, without a serrated edge.

French fries

Homemade thick (or thin) fries. Golden crunchy on the outside, soft on the inside.

Lettuce

Butterhead lettuce with vinaigrette, especially the crunchy leaves from the center.

White bread

For those who like steak with gravy.

Frying

Seared golden brown, over a medium-high heat, with a light crispy crust. Preferably rare (saignant) or medium-rare inside (*bien cuit* is not done).

Fat

Creamy, pale yellow, baked rind of fat for extra flavor.

Gravy

Baking fat in which molten fat from the meat and melted butter are blended together. The perfect base for a rich gravy or sauce.

5 beginner's mistakes

- Poor quality industrial meat
- Wrong frying pan
- Excessive heat while frying
- Fried for too long or too quickly
- Bloodbath on the plate

What is needed for making the Perfect Steak? This is not very complicated, at least for those who know the rules. A short guide in 15 steps, from buying your favorite steak to cutting it and serving it on a plate.

1 *know your steak*

Know what you want. An ordinary steak, succulent tenderloin or striploin? Or something with a trim of fat, like a rib-eye or sirloin? With or without a bone? Or do you want a narrower cut such as porterhouse, thick skirt or brisket (excellent steaks that are not very expensive – see p.64)? What animal did your steak come from really? Angus, Hereford, shorthorn or Texas longhorn? Has the meat been matured, and if so, how long? Ask your organic butcher about this, keep him on his toes. If the look in his eyes is a look of incomprehension, try another butcher. If he does not have your favorite cut available, ask him to cut a fresh piece, with the exact thickness and weight that you want. Do not settle for any less.

2 *buy quality*

Is the meat from a well-bred, free-range animal? Or did it come from a large-scale meat industry where animals are fed with hormones and power feed to force them to reach their maximum slaughter weight in no time at all? And most of all: look at the meat and feel it before you buy it. Meat is often sold while it is too fresh. If it is wet with blood seeping out, vacuum packed in plastic, lying on a moisture absorber in a polystyrene tray, leave it where it is. Not much can be done with this meat and it causes spattering in the pan. Good meat should be rather dull and dry looking and it may be of a dark, deep-red color. The surface feels silky smooth. The tastiest steak is dry-aged for three to four weeks (on the leg), which causes the need to lose some moisture, to become extra tender and to gain more flavor.

Dry-aged meat: minimum
three weeks of maturation

3 *proper pan*

Steaks are seared on a relatively high heat to obtain a nice brown and crispy crust. You therefore need to invest in a good frying pan with a thick bottom, which does not necessarily need to be expensive. The cheapest option available is an iron frying pan (made from sheet metal), Which can become very hot, it has good heat distribution across the base and it does not become warped. When using it for the first time you have to burn the pan in (see p.77). After use, clean with kitchen paper and paint a thin layer of oil on the pan before storing it in the closet (against rust). Alternatively you can buy a more expensive, multiple layer frying pan made from stainless steel with aluminum. Excellent conductivity, heat resistance, dishwasher safe. With the more expensive and heavier pans with a nonstick layer you can also brown a steak reasonably well, but unlike steel and stainless steel, it leaves very little encrustation on the base. This encrustation can be used to make a delicious gravy or sauce.

Also note the size. The butter (and the steak) burn faster in a pan that is too large. It is ideal to leave a space of about a quarter inch between the steaks. An 11 inch frying pan is good for four large steaks. The 9 inch frying pan is good for two steaks, and for only one steak an 8 inch pan is sufficient. A frying pan with an oven-proof handle (not plastic) is also very useful if you want to bake your steak in the oven for a bit.

4 *butter & oil*

Butter gives steak a rich, fatty taste, while olive oil does not provide the same result. The advantage of the olive oil (or any other type of oil such as grape seed oil or sunflower oil), however, is that it has a higher combustion point than butter. This means that the pan can become hotter without the fat burning onto the pan. A high heat is needed for the best searing results. Margarine (fake butter) and liquid cooking fat have a high burning point, but lack the taste of real butter. Some steak chefs therefore prefer to use a mixture of oil and butter. For more taste after searing and and to temper the heat, more butter is added. If you are careful while frying and searing (you do not use excessively high temperatures) you can use only butter or clarified butter. This will give you a nice golden brown, crispy crust and optimum flavor.

Clarified butter

Clarified butter is butter with the milk solids filtered out, which means that it can be used at very high temperatures without burning. Method: melt the butter over a low heat in a steel pan. Scoop the foam from the surface using a spoon or a foam skimmer. Slowly pour the liquid butter into a clean pan and leave the cloudy milk solids behind in the pan. Set the liquid butter apart and allow it to cool to lukewarm. Variant: ghee, Indian clarified butter, which can be bought in a canned form in oriental stores.

5 *before you start frying*

Always allow your steak to reach room temperature to ensure even cooking. Leaving the meat for half an hour or even up to an hour outside of the refrigerator on a cutting board, covered with a sheet of household foil, is not a problem. Do not let meat from the deep freezer thaw on the counter, on a heating tray or in warm water, but lay it covered on a plate in the fridge. This will ensure that bacteria does not have time to develop. Rinse away the leaked meat juices after thawing. Pat your steaks dry with kitchen paper as moisture is the enemy when you want to make a nice crust. Wet meat does not brown well.

6 *steak seasoning*

Before putting a steak in the pan, sprinkle it with salt and pepper. Opinions are divided in culinary circles about whether it is best to put salt on the meat before during or after. Salt is supposed to extract moisture from the meat, which makes it tough and dry. Cookbooks often state that it is therefore better not to pre-salt the meat. Nonsense. Ask any of the better chefs, meat experts and chemists and they will all say the same thing: flavor the meat first. Salt contributes to the development of the taste (including the gravy) while frying. Meat that is pre-salted also browns a little bit easier while frying. Before frying, use a cheaper fine salt (it dissolves in the dripping). Once out of the pan, season with (more expensive) coarse sea salt.

Storage

When covered with foil meat can be kept in the refrigerator for 2 to 3 days. When vacuum-packed the meat can be refrigerated for at least a week. Hermetically sealed steaks can be kept in the freezer for 3 to 6 months. This is handy when you order your meet online or if you order a complete meat package from a farmer. Vacuum-packed meat can discolor when you take it out of the packaging. The color changes from dark red to brighter red when it comes into contact with oxygen. Any strange odors should disappear after a few minutes.

Favorite pan:
steel with thick bottom

7 *searing**

For perfect browning (and therefore also taste) it is necessary to first fry the meat on both sides until brown over a relatively high heat. This is also called searing, which is strictly speaking a misnomer (see The myth of searing on p. 20). Method: Sprinkle the steaks with freshly ground pepper and salt. Preheat the frying pan for 2-3 minutes over a high heat. As soon as the pan is hot (check by dropping a few drops of water in the pan – if the drops scatters and spatters the pan is hot enough), reduce the heat to medium. Put butter in the frying pan and let it bubble (the butter discolors and the foam pulls away). Steaks with more fat, such as rib-eye or sirloin can also be cooked without any oil or butter (unless you want to make a gravy or sauce). Fry your steak on both sides until brown. Steaks with a rind of fat should first be fried on the side with the fat. This will cause the fat to melt and provide extra flavor to the dripping.

* Some professional chefs prefer to preheat the meat in an oven for an hour at a low temperature (120 – 140°F) for about an hour. This also allows the surface of the meat to dry out a little bit more, which promotes the formation of a crust when frying afterwards. Once the meat has reached the desired core temperature (120 – 130° F for medium-rare), the meat can be fried in a frying pan. This will be very fast, 10 to 15 seconds per side, as the meat already has the correct temperature on the inside.

8 *frying:*
   do not move it around too much

A steak can be fried with the meat 'dancing around in the pan', i.e. by turning the meat around often, or a steak can be fried by turning the meat as little as possible, which is only one time. The first option is nice and active: almost like you're trying to say, 'look at me and my steak!', but the second option is the better option. When you continuously turn the meat, the browning process is interrupted, which means that it is more difficult to brown the meat and the taste also does not develop very well.

Listen to your steak

Most cookbooks recommend frying steaks over a high heat, which most people assume to mean that the gas must be at its highest setting. This is not correct and only results in the butter and the steak burning. Blackened on the outside, cold inside. The best is to hit your pan well, but then to keep a close eye on your steak once it is in the pan. Look at your steak and more importantly, listen to it. While frying you must hear a gentle sizzling sound as the juices heat up. Add a bit of butter as soon as the butter threatens to burn (this will cause the dripping and the pan to cool down slightly).

Do's and don'ts for a perfect crust

Moisture on the meat hinders the formation of a thin, crispy and golden brown crust. What is the best way to counter moisture?

- First dab your steak dry with paper towels
- Do not put too many pieces of meat in the pan at once
- Make the pan and the butter or oil as hot as possible
- The hotter and shorter the frying process, the more moisture evaporates in a short time (without overcooking the steak inside) – but be careful not to burn the fat!

9 rare, medium, well done?

The crux of any perfectly cooked steak is to get the correct doneness. Do you prefer rare, medium-rare or well done? The easiest way to determine those is to make a small cut in the steak and to see if the meat is done. Another way, which requires some experience, is to feel it. When the meat is rare it will be soft, but when it is well done it will be firm. A common testing method is to use a thumb and index finger. Method: press the tips of your thumb and index finger of one hand – lightly – against each other. Now push the index finger of the other hand onto the palm of your hand. This is what the *blue rare* should feel like. Now push a thumb against your middle finger and feel again: this is what *rare* should feel like. Now move your thumb to your ring finger: this is what *medium* should feel like. Now push your thumb against your pinkie to feel what *medium well done/well done* should feel like. It is recommended to use a food probe for larger roasts in the oven. They do not work very well with steaks, however, as the probe is too close to the hot pan bottom, which means that it is unreliable.

10 how do you determine the doneness?

The cooking time of a piece of beef depends on its size. Old cookbooks normally state that cooking time depends on the weight (for example, 15 minutes for 1 pound of red meat at 350°F). This is an outdated tip because the weight is less important than the thickness of the meat. A much more reliable method is a food probe. Insert the probe in the center of the piece of meat (not too close to a bone because the temperature around the bone increases more rapidly). Remove the roast from the oven once the correct core temperature is reached. You can check your probe by holding it in boiling water. The temperature should read around 212°F. A beef rib is rare at a core temperature of approximately 120°F. Less tender cuts of meat are normally very good when they are cooked slowly at a low temperature (212°F) and it can sometimes take up to 10 hours before the desired core temperature is reached.

The Maillard reaction

The browning of meat is also known as the Maillard reaction, named after the French chemist Louis Camille Maillard. Heating causes a complex series of chemical reactions. This process does not only create a beautiful golden brown color in your steak, but it also contributes to a rich, full flavor. Maillard browning occurs only with a top temperature of 250 – 280°F. Other products where this reaction also occurs with heating include potatoes (french fries) and onions.

The myth of searing

A popular misconception is that searing off the meat is necessary to keep the precious juices inside. This theory, which was made famous around the world by the German chemist Justus von Liebig (also the inventor of the stock cube) in 1850, has long had a negative effect on cookbook writers and professional chefs. This may sound very plausible, but it is pure nonsense as the American Harold McGee, a leading culinary journalist and researcher, proved in a convincing fashion. The crust of a steak is not waterproof. Even an amateur chef can easily observe this fact. The sizzling noise in the pan is the sound of meat juices that escape continuously. In fact: the higher the heat while searing, the more the meat dries out (this is also why the temperature has to be turned down after searing). This is no reason not to sear, however, as searing promotes the taste.

BLUE RARE/ BLEU

Seared, (almost) raw, 100%
bloody-red and warm inside
113°F
COOKING TIME:
1 minute on each side

RED (RARE)/ SAIGNANT

Seared, 75% bloody-red and 120°F
in the middle
COOKING TIME:
1.5 – 2 minutes per side

MEDIUM/ À POINT

Seared, 25% red-pink on the inside,
130 – 140°F
COOKING TIME:
3-4 minutes per side

MEDIUM WELL/ BIEN CUIT

Seared, slightly pink on the inside,
150°F
COOKING TIME:
5 minutes per side

WELL DONE

160°F, seared
100% brown inside
COOKING TIME:
5 minutes per side

* Another common category
is medium-rare: this is
strictly between red (rare)/
saignant and medium/
à point. Or: seared, 50%
bloody-red inside, 120-130°F
(about 3 minutes per side).
Also used: very rare (bleu
froid), 104°F. The steak is
browned on the outside and
100% red and still cold
inside.

* Cooking times are estimates, based on a steak
  of about ¾ to 1 inch thick.
  The thicker the steak, the longer the cooking time.

11 letting it rest

Meat (a piece of muscle) contracts once it is heated. To ensure that the meat is appropriately tender after frying it is necessary to let the steak rest for a while. This will allow the juices to return to the meat, which will let the meat relax and prevent a bloodbath when you cut the meat. It is best to let the meat rest for five minutes, loosely wrapped in aluminum foil in the shape of a tunnel or a tent, with two open ends so that the steam can escape. If the steam is trapped in the crispy crust will become soft again. Ideally the meat should be left to rest on a grill, e.g. a roasting rack, with a tray or a plate at the bottom to collect the juices.

12 making a sauce or gravy

The same basic principles apply to nearly every sauce. Method: after frying the steak, remove the excess dripping from the pan and set one or two tablespoons of dripping and encrustations aside (a lot of flavor is contained in here). Fry some seasoning such as chopped shallots, carrots or other vegetables in the dripping until soft. Pour some liquid in the pan (such as wine or broth) and scrape the encrustation from the base. The mixture will steam and sizzle (this is known as deglazing). Reduce the liquid as necessary. Stir in the meat juices that are released while resting for extra flavor. Allowed to simmer for a while. Use a wire whisk to whisk in lumps of ice-cold butter, piece by piece. Wait until a lump has melted and blended in before adding the next one to the pan. The butter binds the sauce and provides a full flavor. If you want to make gravy, cool down the hot pan by adding a few spoons of hot water. Allow to simmer over a medium heat to create a nice, thick brown gravy.

13 dry aging

Dry aging is the ripening of meat on the bone under controlled conditions in a cold room with approximately 85% air humidity, air circulation, and with a temperature between 32 and 33°F. During this dry aging process – which takes at least 21 days – up to thirty percent of the moisture in the meat evaporates. This is the process of slow dying where the enzymes present break down the muscle tissue. This gives the meat a very soft texture and intense flavor. The meat is not ready for consumption when it comes out of the dry aging process. It feels hard and dry and looks a little bit black on the outside. This natural black crust protects the meat during ripening against drying and bacterial growth. The butcher then cuts the crust from the meat to give it a 'clean' look and he removes the bone. When you cut the dry-aged meat through you will find that it is bright red and as soft as butter on the inside. Until recently dry-aged steaks were only sold to restaurants, but this top-quality meat is increasingly becoming available for everyone at a select few butchers and through online stores.

14 a good knife & cutting

Use a sharp and smooth blade without any serrations. If you use a blunt and/or serrated knife you will end up with a bloodbath on the plate (try it yourself if you want). Good restaurants always provide you with a separate smooth table knife when you order a steak. When cutting a complete roast, use a very sharp carving knife. Cut into thick or thin slices, as preferred (traditionally thin is considered to be slightly fancier). Cut against the grain. What is the grain? If you look closely at the meat you will see that there are lines running down it. You have to cut right along these lines. The reason is that when you cut along the long fibers the meat is easier to chew.

15 side dishes

The perfect steak is a meal in itself, But you can also eat it with crispy golden steak fries or with white bread (to mop up the gravy or sauce). A meal fit for a king. Colorful vegetables always do well on the plate and they also go well with your steak. Classic examples are crispy cabbage lettuce or roasted vine tomatoes. See recipe suggestions elsewhere in this book.

Fake aged meat

Many butchers and, increasingly, supermarkets are selling boneless vacuum-packed meat that they have imported from various parts of the world, which they then sell as 'ripe' meat. This is a misleading term. This meat is wrapped in plastic, which which means that it does become ripe, but also sour. Maturing while vacuum-packed is called wet-aging. Sometimes the meat is taken from the packaging and hung in a drying cabinet for a while, after which it is sold as dry-aged. This is pure fraud. The difference is in the taste as wet-aged meat loses considerably less moisture, which means that it is not as flavorful as real dry-aged beef.

STEAK

FROM FIELD TO TABLE

The
animal

Scotbeef slaughterhouse in Bridge of Allan,
Stirling, Central Scotland

Know your cattle

Which animal did your steak come from? Race is a determining factor in the flavor of your steak. Some races literally have more fat on the bones than others. Some animals are bred purely for their meat, while others are intended for milk production or for both. What breeds of cattle are mostly available at the better butchers and restaurants in the Netherlands?

Fat is an important factor in the taste. According to nutrition researchers fat contributes to more than one third of the tenderness, juiciness and flavor of a steak. The more fat, the richer the taste (personal preference is naturally the decisive factor). Besides the fat on the outside, the fat within the steak is particularly important. The fat marbling (thin white lines), also known as intramuscular fat, has a beneficial effect on the taste.

The degree of fat and meat development in cattle is determined by two factors: race and feed. Some races are more prone to fat than others. Also, the conditions under which the animal is kept play an important role. Was the animal given sufficient time to become ready for slaughter? Was the animal free range and allowed to graze in the meadow? Did it consume a natural diet? Was it fattened and, if so, what additional nutritional was provided? Perhaps more important: was the transport from the farmer to the abattoir and the actual slaughtering process of the animal completed with as little stress as possible?

Age
American beef mainly comes from cattle between 15 and 24 months old. In Europe it was assumed until recently that meat from an animal that is less than two years old would not have much taste. Real quality comes from adult animals that are three to four years old. Since the BSE crisis, regulations are in place in most European countries that require cattle that is older than thirty months to undergo BSE tests before they are slaughtered as the risk of BSE increases as the animal gets older. Meat sold in Europe is therefore these days mostly from younger cattle, no older than 30 months. Older cattle, such as 'retired' dairy cows, are less palatable as they have more connective tissue and the meat is therefore tougher.

Diet
Age and diet are closely intertwined. The earlier an animal reaches the desired slaughter weight, the more economical it is for the producer. Rapid, forest growth does not always mean good quality, however. Grass-fed cattle do not gain weight as quickly and they take longer to become ready for slaughter. Grass eaters usually produce tastier meat than cattle that are fed with grain or concentrated feed. Grass, clover, buttercups and herbs provide an earthy and pronounced flavor, supplemented by grass silage in the winter months (dry, preserved grass). To get cattle ready for slaughter at a younger age most farmers feed their cattle with grains such as maize and barley. These grains lead to faster meat and fat growth and after about 15 to 24 months they are ready for slaughter. Their meat has a slightly tender, but less pronounced flavor than grass-fed beef. Good cattle spend a major part of their lives in the meadow, before they are fattened for a short period of 3 to 4 months.

Unfortunately this is not always the case. In the wholesale meat industry in countries such as the United States and Australia, cattle are raised on huge barren sand plains (known as feedlots) where juicy pastures are hard to find. To force rapid growth (more meat and fat growth) these animals are given a daily diet of grains, soy and (sometimes chemical) growth promoters. This is not what can be considered a natural diet or honest meat. Wagyu cattle are fattened in a very special manner. These cattle, originally from Japan, are given a special diet to make them ready to be slaughtered, which provides strongly marbled and very tasty meat.

Weight

The maximum natural slaughter weight differs significantly with each race. Some well-known giant breeds of cattle include Belgian Blue, Charolais and Chianina from Italy. With these races the females can reach a slaughter weight of more than 2000 pounds (weight after slaughter of 1100 – 1300 pounds). Smaller varieties include Aberdeen Angus and Hereford, which can grow up to a maximum of 1500 pounds (slaughter weight of 650 to 750 pounds). Big animals provide big steaks. Côte de boeuf from a Belgian Blue is larger than from an Aberdeen Angus. When it comes to taste these big ones do not give way to the smaller races, as the meat loving Belgians and Italians have known for many years. In the Dutch hospitality industry there is a preference for smaller breeds, however. South American cattle, for instance (mostly Aberdeen Angus and Hereford hybrids), yield perfectly portioned steaks from 8 – 9 ounces.

Dairy cows

The race is of relatively minor importance when it comes to quality. Consumers often do not know if their meat came from cows or bulls. In the Netherlands most of the meat comes from cows, such as heifers (cows that have never had calves). The situation is very different in countries such as the United States and the United Kingdom, where bulls and steers are dominant. It is not easy to show the difference, but many meat connoisseurs nevertheless have strong preferences.

Cows are slightly softer and they have more fat, while bulls have less fat, which makes them attractive in the industry as consumers generally prefer lean rather than fatty meat. Bulls also grow faster. In many other countries steers (castrated bulls) are also very popular as they are quieter than bulls, they have less male hormones and they have more fat, the same as cows.

The vast majority of the cattle in meadows in the Netherlands are milk cows, such as Holstein-Friesian. Foreign types of cattle, often bred by enthusiastic hobby farmers, are on a modest rise, such as Limousin, Hereford and Charolais. These races even have their own national pedigree in the Netherlands in which accurate records are kept of the ancestries of an animal. The purpose of the pedigree is to keep the race pure.

The best-known type of cattle in the Netherlands

The best-known type of cattle in the Netherlands is the black and white Holstein-Friesian (also known as *zwartbont*). These cattle make up approximately 70 – 75% of all cattle in the Netherlands (the red variety is called Red Holstein-Friesian). The breed originated from a Frisian-Dutch race which used to be the most popular dairy cow in the world as it provides both milk and meat (a dual purpose race). Holstein-Friesian is primarily used for milk production, but also for meat. Cheap beef normally comes from older and dry Holsteiners. Butchers often say that they are good for ground beef and sausages, but they do not produce good quality steaks.

Look at the head!

Some types of cattle are bred purely for milk, while others are bred purely for meat production, such as Aberdeen Angus, Hereford and Limousin. How do you tell the difference? Look at the head. A long head with many veins is typical of a dairy breed, while races with a distinctive short, broad head and firmer legs are normally bred for meat.

SCOTTISH INTERNATIONAL
Aberdeen Angus

Scotland

Originally from the region around Aberdeen in Northeast Scotland. A very distinctive feature of this race is a head without any horns. They are very popular among connoisseurs as they produce rich and marbled meat. Aberdeen Angus is widely used for crossbreeding with other races to optimize milk or meat production and is currently being bred all around the world. There are different pedigrees in various countries in which the bloodlines and origin are defined.

BELGIAN BODYBUILDER
Belgian Blue

Belgium

These cattle are also called Belgian Blue-White, Belgian White and Blue Pied. The pride of Belgium. Distinguishing features: strongly muscled, broad back and thick hindquarters with blue or black spots. They are called the bodybuilder among beef cattle because of the rapid and extensive meat accretion. The calves are so large that they are often delivered by Caesarean section. The meat is relatively lean, with little fat cover.

OLD RACE
Blaarkop

The Netherlands

This type of cattle is not very common in the Netherlands (only about 2% of the national livestock), but it is a very old and robust breed. The name *Blaarkop* is Dutch and it means blister head, due to the white head with characteristic black (or red) rings around the eyes (blisters). They are originally from Groningen, but also have a dominant present in the Green Heart. Suitable for organic milk and meat.

NICE BLONDE
Blonde d'Aquitaine

Southwest France

Originally from Southwest France, but now also common in a few other countries. Characteristics: typical blonde, light pink color, with strong shoulders and large hindquarters. This is a relatively young race that first got its own pedigree in 1962, and it has also been recognized with a Dutch pedigree since 1982. Its meat has a fine structure which is very popular among skilled French chefs due to its tenderness.

FAST GROWER
Charolais

France

This is one of the fastest growing breeds of cattle. Suitable for both milk and meat. Due to its great yields Charolais is one of the most common types of cattle in Europe and they are found in more than 70 countries. A bull can weigh as much as 2400, while a cow can weigh up to 2000 pounds. Originally from France, around Charolles in Burgundy. Distinguishing features: creamy white fur and a pink nose.

ITALY'S FINEST
Chianina

Italy

Exclusive race. Very popular in Tuscany and Umbria popular because of Bistecca alla Fiorentina (see the recipe on page 110) for which the Italians only use Chianina. Also known as "il gigantismo" in Italy, which means gigantic. Bulls can reach a shoulder height of more than 6 feet and weigh up to 3700 pounds. Distinguishing feature: porcelain-white color. Chianina has an original and controlled name of origin and its meat is only available at quality butcheries.

WITH OR WITHOUT HORNS?
Hereford
Herefordshire, Wales

Popular meat breed, originally from Herefordshire, Wales. Very popular in North America, Australia and Great Britain. Can be slaughtered at a relatively young age, with nice fat. Is often used for crossbreeding with Aberdeen Angus and Wagyu. Distinguishing features: powerfully built, red (brown) color with a white or speckled head and white stripe on the neck. The Polled Hereford is a variant without horns.

WITH A WHITE BAND
Lakenvelder
The Netherlands

Centuries old, critically endangered breed that is busy re-emerging. Completely red or black cattle from the Netherlands with distinctive broad white band between the shoulder and hip. The front and hind legs are both red or black. Three-quarters of the animals is motley black, while the rest is red. A well built animal, which is a bit smaller than most livestock breeds. Suitable for both milk and meat (dual purpose breed).

RACE WITH CLASS
Limousin
France

Along with Charolais this is one of the best-known beef breeds. Originally from the French region of Limoges. Characteristic reddish-brown coat with light circles around the eyes and nose. The breed is used in the Netherlands for meat production and for nature conservation. Limousin – very lean meat – is a regular on the menus at classy restaurants. The Netherlands also has its own Limousin pedigree.

ANIMAL WITH BITE
Meuse-Rhine-Issel
The Netherlands

Traditional meat breed from the Netherlands, originally from the region along the rivers Meuse, Issel and Rhine. About 15-20% of all cattle in the Netherlands are of MRI origin. With its red-and-white color it looks a little bit like the motley red Holstein-Friesian, but it has stronger legs and thicker back and hindquarters. Suitable for both meat and milk production. Fine structure with a firm bite.

MOUNTAIN CATTLE
Simmental
Switzerland

Originally from Switzerland, popular in the Jura and the Alps. Produces milk for Emmental and Gruyère, but also has a good reputation as a meat breed. Appearance: white head with golden yellow to red colored coat. This breed dates back to the Middle Ages and it has one of the oldest pedigrees (since 1806). The meat has a nice covering of fat, a fine structure and it is well marbled with intramuscular fat.

ROLLS-ROYCE AMONG CATTLE
Wagyu
Japan

Wagyu beef is of Japanese origin and of exceptional quality ("wa" means Japanese and "gyu" cattle). In times gone by only the Emperor of Japan was allowed to eat this unique high-quality beef, but since the 90s Wagyu beef has also been available outside of Japan. Known for superior marbling of intramuscular fat and a rich flavor. The meat is quite pricey and is only available at a select few butcheries.

Wagyu Farm *De Drie Morgen*,
Spijkerboor, the Netherlands

Wagyu
in the meadow

Wagyu cattle, originally from Japan, have a legendary reputation. They are the most pampered cattle on earth as they enjoy massages and are fed with beer. The prices for Wagyu meat are just as legendary as you can expect to pay around $35 per ounce. Marketing hype? I paid a visit to the Wagyu farm *De Drie Morgen* **in the Netherlands where thoroughbred Wagyu grazed in the meadow in the natural area near Purmerend.**

Every morning at 7:00 am, Rob Baarsma, owner and founder of the farm De Drie Morgen, gets into his steel boat for the daily inspection of his cattle. In this traditional Dutch nature reserve of Wormer- en Jisperveld, in the town Spijkerboor, near Purmerend, which is no more than 9 miles from the center of Amsterdam, his beloved cows are grazing peacefully in the meadow. Spread out over a few different islands, which are accessible only by boat, the jet-black silhouettes of these impressive muscular animals can be seen against the horizon. "When the bulls get into their heat cycle they jump into the water," said Baarsma as he stood at the helm. "Nothing holds them back. They simply swim to the other side looking for females." The farmer therefore checks every morning to see if any of the animals got into trouble in the water during their nocturnal escapades.

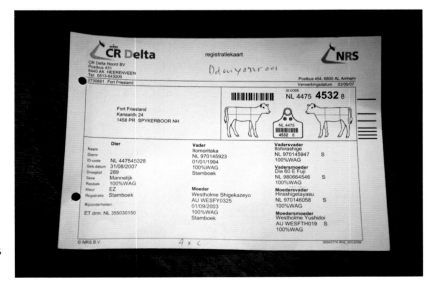

Certification of 100% purebred Wagyu: Japanese ancestors

The Islands of De Drie Morgen
in the natural area of
Wormer- en Jisperveld

Ancestors

The animals in this peaceful meadow are not just any type of cattle, but cattle of the famous Wagyu breed. This is also not a type crossbred with Wagyu, but – and this is unique – one hundred percent pure Wagyu, direct descendants of Japanese ancestry. In 2003 Baarsma, a former project developer, started his Wagyu adventure. "I wanted to have a more peaceful life, so I bought an old farmhouse in some land. To cover the area with grass in a sustainable manner, I needed some cattle. When I heard about the prices and opportunities with Wagyu beef, I thought: Why not combine nature conservation and livestock?" His wife Caroline, a former European champion in equestrian sports, had extensive experience in horse breeding. It all started with a first calf, but the herd now numbers about 150 authentic Wagyu cattle. The quality of his cattle is unmistakable, say Wagyu connoisseurs. Even foreign breeders come to buy Wagyu breeding bulls from him.

Beer

The mystique surrounding this legendary Japanese creature is legendary, and celebrity chefs around the world are full of praise for the meat that is marbled with intramuscular fat and the rich, full-fat taste of the meat. The price also reflects this as you can pay up to $35 for an ounce of the ultimate in pure Wagyu beef. The stories of cows in Japan that enjoy massages and are fed beer to achieve top quality meat are well known. Is it just the marketing hype, or are these stories true? Baarsma: "The stories are correct, but for different reasons than people imagine. In Japan land for cattle is very hard to come by. Most of the land is devoted to rice growing because the Japanese government wishes to provide for all of its own rice needs. In Japan these animals have very little space available, almost similar to the space that our boxed calves used to have. They hardly have any space to move. In order to stimulate their blood flow it is therefore necessary to massage them with hemp gloves and brushes. They also sometimes given beer to arouse their appetites."

At Baarsma's stables the cattle also enjoy massages, but here it is mostly for self-indulgent reasons. The cattle clearly enjoy it as they drool with pleasure as they scrape against the hard massage brushes that are fitted to the stables. "Wagyu are very sensitive to stress," explained Baarsma. "That is why we want to create a pleasant, quiet environment for them. That helps to promote the quality of the meat."

His animals are also spoiled in other ways. They lie on a bed of straw that is decomposing at the bottom, which creates heat of up to 120°F, so it is almost like they have their own electric blankets. During the few months before they are slaughtered the cattle enjoy a sophisticated diet to fatten them up. The diet consists of hay that is rich in natural grass, wheat and barley – without growth agents or antibiotics, ensures Baarsma – but he does not want to provide exact details. "It is a secret recipe from Japan," said the farmer. The food and the calm environment are partly responsible for the unique taste of the meat. Also outside in the country the cattle enjoy a good life as 150 animals graze on 250 acres of land – 0.6 animals per acre. For the first two years of their lives they mostly graze outside if the weather permits. During the third year they stay permanently in the stable as they are fattened with hay and dry feed to ensure that they are ready to be slaughtered at 36 months. Slaughtering – a major stress factor for the cattle – is done in the vicinity, which means that the journey time is limited.

The Wagyu of De Drie Morgen enjoy massages with rough brushes

Embryos

It is a small miracle that Baarsma managed to get a hold of a thoroughbred Wagyu herd in the Netherlands. Wagyu cattle are originally from Japan and their export is currently officially banned. There was only a very small window in history where the export of live Wagyu was permitted (see further on). There are only a few Wagyu breeders in Europe, and most of them only have crossbred Wagyu variants.

In 2005 Baarsma successfully managed to buy thoroughbred Wagyus embryos from a breeder friend of his in Australia, which he then imported to the Netherlands. The Australian father and mother of this embryo – as stated in the detailed registration document, including a nose print – came directly from thoroughbred Wagyu cattle from the middle of the 90s, at which time they were exceptionally allowed to be exported from Japan.

An old Dutch surrogate ensured that the first Wagyu calf was born on Dutch soil nine months later. "That was a very special moment," recalled Baarsma. He was baptized Shogun 1 and he has proven to be a breeding bull with very strong genes. That massive bull (with the number 4242 on a yellow badge in his ear) is still in the stables at De Drie Morgen where he is enjoying his retirement. By buying other known bloodlines and by employing techniques such as artificial insemination and in vitro fertilization (IVF or test tube fertilization) the unique Dutch Wagyu cattle was bred with patience and dedication, to their current numbers.

Breeding bull Shogun 1 has been a very good financial asset as his sperm is sold at Euro 40 per tube. De Drie Morgen also sells embryos to other breeders (an embryo sells for around Euro 1000 over the counter). Together with the sale of livestock for slaughter and breeding this is one of the main sources of income at De Drie Morgen.

Owner Rob Baarsma
inspects his cattle by boat
every morning

On average one cattle goes to the slaughterhouse per week.

Fake Wagyu

Most Wagyu beef sold in the Netherlands and the rest of Europe at top restaurants is actually not permitted to be sold under the name Wagyu. The reason for those is that the meat is often not Wagyu beef, but rather from crossbreeding, which means that it is not 100% thoroughbred. "Consumers often do not know exactly what they get when they ask for Wagyu beef, but they still pay a premium price, as if the meat is real Wagyu," said Baarsma. "But the difference between the taste of Wagyu from crossbreeding and the taste of a thoroughbred Wagyu is unmistakable."

De Drie Morgen is therefore calling for a type of label that clearly identifies thoroughbreds Wagyu, as is the case in Australia. Well-known chefs who serve the meat at their restaurants, such as Sergio Herman of Oud Sluis and Peter Goossens of Hof van Cleve in Belgium, state that their Wagyu meat comes from one hundred percent thoroughbred Wagyus.

How to prepare Wagyu beef

Wagyu is especially known for the highly refined marbling of the intramuscular fat in the meat. Wagyu cattle are not slaughtered at an age earlier than two to three years, which means that the meat takes up to twice as long to prepare as other meats. A sophisticated diet during the last year of the life of the animal contributes to the unmistakable rich flavor. The precious Wagyu meat therefore deserves to be prepared with great care. Butter or oil is hardly necessary when baking as the meat contains enough fat on its own. Wagyu beef should be cooked over a moderate to medium heat. The fat marbling in the meat has a low melting point (around 90°F). The trick is to keep the fat in the meat after cooking it to take full advantage of a few special properties of the meat. Wagyu beef is available for sale at quality butcheries throughout the country.

Wagyu worldwide

Wagyu is a Japanese breed of cattle ('wa' means Japanese and 'gyu' means beef) which is one of the most exclusive meat varieties in the world. Up to the present day there has been an export ban on Wagyu cattle in Japan (also known as Kobe beef). There have only been a few exceptions in the past where export of a few animals was permitted to the United States and to Australia for reasons that included scientific research. Towards the end of the 90s a breeding program was started outside of Japan with thoroughbred Wagyu cattle. Wagyu meat that is currently for sale in Europe comes from farms outside of Japan, such as De Drie Morgen. The breeding laboratory for Wagyu throughout the world is Australia where they currently have 80,000 of the cattle. Often this is not one hundred percent thoroughbred Wagyu, but hybrids with Hereford and Aberdeen Angus cattle.

Report:
Aberdeen Angus,
a global brand

Netherton Farm,
Blackford, Auchterarder, Scotland

Aberdeen Angus has become synonymous with good quality steak throughout the world during the last few decades. This deep black and exceedingly strong cattle is originally from Aberdeen in Scotland.

On the Netherton Farm, near Edinburgh, they have one of the oldest Aberdeen Angus herds in Scotland. The first member of the herd on this family farm dates back a few generations to 1924. Currently there are approximately 80 thoroughbred Aberdeen Angus cattle walking around on the farm of the McLaren family. These animals are not intended for the slaughterhouse, but for breeding. The McLarens enjoy a good reputation and their legendary breeding bull Netherton Figo was sold in 2005 for a record amount of Euro 35,000. This bull has an above average libido and seed quality, qualities that all breeders prefer. Within a few years the fortunate buyer got three times that amount back through the sale of superior sperm and by taking advantage of its considerable mating talent.

Breeding bull

Black Kiwi looked on curiously from his stall, filled with fresh hay, at the visitor entering Netherton, while William McLaren Jr. lovingly stroked his nose. "Curiosity is embedded in the genes of the Aberdeen Angus," said William, who co-owns the farm with his father, William Sr. The bull, not yet two years old, is impressively large and it looks a little dangerous with the traditional ring in its nose. Its shoulder stands almost five feet above the ground and it weighs roughly 2,200 pounds. William comments approvingly about this bull: "Look at its beautiful, broad back. We like that, because that's the most expensive meat where you cut steaks from. It also has a strong back length, which is good for large sirloin. It also has very firm hindquarters." Black Kiwi will soon be

**Aberdeen Angus breeders
William McLaren senior (left) and junior**

sold on the bull auction, where William hopes he will get Euro 5,000 for his bull.

Food chain

"We breeders are at the top of the food chain," explained William. "The decisions we make now determine what consumers will have on their plates in about eight years' time." This is a reference to the essence of the breeder's work: breeding the finest Aberdeen Angus males and females, with the aim of obtaining juicy and tender meat with the right taste and fat marbling. For outsiders this seems to be a wondrous world of bloodlines, IVF and frozen embryos.

From the cradle of Scotland, the birthplace of the original Aberdeen Angus breed, the race has spread to all parts of the world, from New Zealand to Brazil. Although the small scale of the rural farm Netherton may suggest otherwise, the McLaren family is active on a global scale. William Jr.: "We travel from Australia to South America, looking for

the best Mr. Universe." Black Kiwi's mother is a famous traditional Scottish bull from the Blackbird family, but his father is a bull with New Zealand genes. Black Kiwi's sister recently won another main prize at one of the many shows in Scotland where regional breeders show their livestock in the knowledge that winners are worth more money.

Studbook

The name 'Aberdeen Angus' is protected. Like other cattle breeds the descendants of true thoroughbred Aberdeen Angus cattle are registered in the national studbook. The Scottish Aberdeen Angus dates back as far as the eighteenth century. The bull Old Jock had the honor of being the first animal to be included in the Aberdeen Angus studbook in 1824. All of the descendants can be traced back to this lineage holder. Also the history of the ancestors of these cattle at Netherton dates back more than a

All Aberdeen Angus cattle can be traced back to the sire Old Jock, 1824

Butcher Johan van Uden (left) inspects the best Aberdeen Angus on location

Black Kiwi bull,
born on the Netherton farm

Burnshot Farm, Braes family

hundred years, which breeders such as the McLarens are very proud of.

Bloodline

Apart from race and bloodline the diet of the animals is a determining factor in the quality of the beef. The Scottish blue 'Scotch Beef' label has acquired PGI status from the European Union, just like Scotch Lamb. The Protected Geographical Indication is a guarantee of origin, which is similar to what happens with Parma Ham and Parmigiano Reggiano. Only Aberdeen Angus that are raised on Scottish farms that meet the strictest PGI control requirements (e.g. animal welfare, diet, transportation) are eligible for the official Scotch Beef quality brand.

The cattle at Netherton have access to vast grazing fields. Jet black Aberdeen Angus cattle, which stand out because of their hornless heads, can be seen everywhere in the Scottish countryside. They are outdoor nearly all year round and they eat thirty to forty different species of grass and herbs, which is a rich and varied diet that is also one hundred percent natural. They are not given additional supplements until a few months before they have reached slaughtering age. This is given to them in the form of barley, wheat and other grains to add a little fat to the meat. Grass feeding contributes significantly to the highly acclaimed rich, unique flavor of the Aberdeen Angus beef.

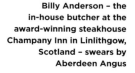

Billy Anderson – the in-house butcher at the award-winning steakhouse Champany Inn in Linlithgow, Scotland – swears by Aberdeen Angus

At the abattoir

The slaughtering method greatly depends on the quality of the meat. Stress hormones are released in cattle that is slaughtered under stressful conditions, which has an adverse effect on the quality of the meat. A sudden increase in the pH values in the muscle can result in the meat becoming dark, tough and dry. Transportation and treatment of the animal at the abattoir are both factors that increase stress. "Slaughtering is not pleasant, but it is necessary," explained Simon Dowling, director of Scotbeef. Scotbeef is a modern abattoir in Scotland that meets the stringent requirements of Scotch Beef. "We do everything within our power to make the process as stress free as possible."

On average about two thousand Scottish cattle pass through the state-of-the-art slaughtering line at Scotbeef. After a farmer from the vicinity has selected cattle to be slaughtered, the cattle is delivered to the abattoir after a brief journey by road. The animals are then given time to get used to the new environment in a large barn with straw and clean drinking water. A veterinarian inspects the passports and medical documents of the animals. There are no screaming employees or animals that are getting whipped around here. The use of prods is prohibited. It is a conscious decision to have few employees on location in order to minimize the stress for the animals. The cattle are led with a gentle hand, one by one, through a tunnel to the killing area, which is a platform that is

not immediately visible. The stunner shoots a pen from a cylinder gun through the head of the animal with the touch of a button, which causes the animal to be brain-dead on impact. The dead animal is then immediately dispatched to the slaughter line where the head is cut off to allow blood to drain from the animal for one minute. The butchers stand on hydraulic platforms along the fully automated line where each is responsible for a specific part of the slaughter process: head, feet, organs, skin, so that only a carcass remains, which is vertically split into two parts. Independent grading masters (not employed at the abattoir) check the entire process to make sure that the appropriate procedures and hygienic standards are followed. The quality of the passing carcasses is evaluated with the naked eye, based on factors such as fat cover. The finest specimens are given an E or U rating, while the lesser ones are given a P or C rating. The hall with

the butchers is located in another section of the slaughterhouse where dozens of skilled butchers work at a considerable tempo as they cut the carcasses into parts. Before boning the meat, the carcasses are suspended in a cold room, under controlled conditions, where they are matured to promote the tenderness and quality of the meat. The in-house butchers wear chainmail aprons and their hands are protected by steel gloves because a slip with the razor-sharp knives that they use could lead to some nasty accidents. The carcasses are cut into rib-eyes, T-bone steaks and tenderloins, as well as some less common cuts. The meat is then ready to be packed as per the specifications of the client (butcher, supermarket, department store, wholesaler) and shipped out. Scottish Aberdeen Angus that had been grazing peacefully in the fields only one week ago are then on their way to the plates of consumers.

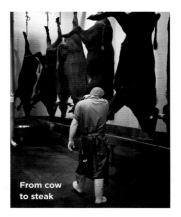

From cow to steak

STEAK

FROM FIELD TO TABLE

The
meat

Know your steak

Where are all the different parts? And which is the most delicious, the loveliest and the best? A mini-lecture on the anatomy of cattle.

Meat consists of muscles and muscles are meant for movement, some more than others. This same principle also applies to cattle muscles. Simply put, there are only two kinds of meat: tender and tough. Tender meat comes from muscles that are rarely used, such as the back, while tough meat comes from muscles that are frequently used, such as the shoulder, neck and legs. Generally speaking, the further away from the hooves and horns, the more tender the meat.

Tough meat contains high levels of connective tissue and only becomes tender after extensive cooking, e.g. stewing in wine for a few hours. Tender meat such as steaks does not need to be cooked for long as it contains less connective tissue. Butchers normally tenderize lower quality meat in order to be able to sell it by pricking the meat with a sharp knife. This destroys the structure, which makes the meat easier to chew. When cutting tenderized meat an excessive amount of blood is released. This inferior quality of steak can be easily identified by the little holes on top.

Quality

Good-quality steak does not need to be treated in this brutal fashion. Tougher meat is not, by definition, of lesser quality, but it is cheaper. Work meat often has more flavor and character than 'lazy' muscles (such as the tenderloin). You can cook some very good steaks from certain types of work meat, such as the porterhouse (located at the muzzle) or escalope (shoulder).

Most steaks come from the back, including the rib, the thin and thick flank, the line of the back, sirloin, rib-eye and T-bone steak. The closer to the rear, the less tender the meat. The most popular meat is always lean as most consumers think that it is risky to consume fat. Fat this the one factor that actually provides the meat with the most flavor. Sirloin steak and rib-eye have a rim of fat on the outside and beautiful fat marbling in the flesh, which is thin white or pale yellow lines of fat (especially in the rib-eye), which looks nice and it is also delicious as the fat melts into the meat to make it nice and juicy.

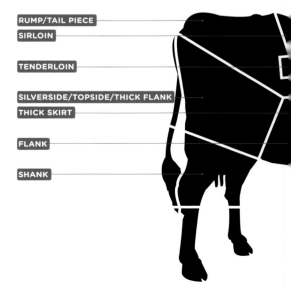

RUMP/TAIL PIECE

SIRLOIN

TENDERLOIN

SILVERSIDE/TOPSIDE/THICK FLANK

THICK SKIRT

FLANK

SHANK

Differences

Each country has its own butcher's culture and boning methods: French butchers cut meat differently from their Dutch counterparts. The same applies to American butchers. What is a very common cut in one country (e.g. bavette in France or porterhouse in the United States) is not known or rare in other countries. Just walk into an average French butchery or supermarket and you would be amazed at all the different names they use for the meat. The differences are also not only national, but also regional: a butcher from Paris bones differently from a butcher in Marseille. In the overview in this chapter the most common names and translations are used.

What makes meat tough?

Muscle tissues are surrounded by a mucous membrane, which bundles different parts together. This membrane is also known as connective tissue. The connective tissues are tied together at the end with white strands, which are known as the tendons. The tendons connect the muscles to the bones. The less connective tissue and tendons, the more tender the meat. When meat that contains connective tissue is cooked for a long time, this tissue becomes gelatin, which makes tough meat soft and very tasty. A good example is braised beef.

How red is red?

Some of the meat available in supermarkets or at your local butcher may appear to have an unnaturally bright red color. This could be due to the use of sophisticated lighting, but but it could also be the result of powders applied to the meat to give it a brighter red color. Check the packaging (or ask the butcher in person): the ingredients listed must be meat only, without any preservatives. What else do I need to look out for when I buy steak?

- **COLOR:** you can recognize good-quality meat from the deep red color
- **COLOR:** animals that were fed a diet that consisted mostly of grains will have pale-yellow fat. Grass-fed cattle will have creamy white fat.
- **LOOK:** the meat must not be damp and it must not lie in a puddle of blood
- **LOOK:** the meat must not seem to be too dry (also look at the edges) and it must have a slight sheen
- **FEEL:** the meat must not be too flaccid; when you push raw meat with your finger there must be some resistance
- **FAT:** deep and rich fat marbling in the meat and a nice fat cover on the outside is important for rib-eye and sirloin, for example
- **STRUCTURE:** the finer the thread, the more tender and softer the meat

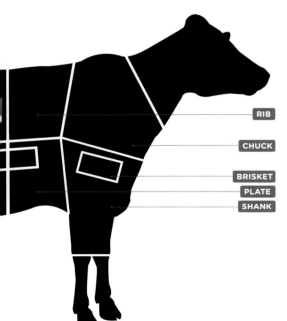

RIB

CHUCK

BRISKET

PLATE

SHANK

Tenderloin

Also known as beef fillet, the tenderloin is the softest and also the most expensive piece of beef That is taken from the elongated muscle inside the loin. This muscle is hardly used, so the meat is extra tender. An average carcass (from an average cow) of 780 pounds only includes about 7 to 9 pounds of tenderloin. This piece of meat contains very subtle fat marbling and it is so soft that you almost can cut it with a fork. The flavor is not very pronounced. Suitable for making carpaccio and beef roast.

OTHER NAMES:
FILET MIGNON (FRENCH),
BEEF FILLET (UK)
PRICE: $ $ $ $
PLACE: FILLET

Chateaubriand

A piece of tenderloin that butchers usually cut from the thick center of the fillet. This is actually not correct, because the chateaubriand is strictly speaking a protrusion at the top of the tenderloin, which is 1 – 1 ½ inches thick and weighs about 13 ounces. It is normally served in a restaurant for two people, which is why it is sometimes identified as a 'double fillet steak'. According to culinary folklore, this piece of meat is named after the French writer and politician François René de Chateaubriand (1768-1848).

OTHER NAMES:
FILET DE BOEUF (FRANCE)
PRICE: $ $ $ $
PLACE: FILLET

Filet mignon

Cut from the middle section and the (smaller) end of the tenderloin. To be cut as a turret (1 ½ – 2 inches thick, 7 – 8 ounces) or a flatter piece (depending on what part of the fillet is used). Some restaurants serve smaller pieces of filet mignon (6 ounces), which they call lady-steaks. The meat is very tender, but it contains relatively little flavor. Filet mignon can also be deformed when the butcher ties a string around it.

OTHER NAMES:
TOURNEDOS (FRANCE),
TENDERLOIN (U.S.),
FILLET (FRANCE, U.S.)
PRICE: $ $ $ $
PLACE: FILLET

Sirloin

This meat comes from the (thinner) loin, which is an extension of the back. Typically it has a rind of fat on the side (good to fry first for extra flavor). A sirloin with a bone is also known as prime rib. Typically it contains fine fat marbling (but less than the rib-eye), which gives it much flavor.

Rib-eye

Oval in shape, with clear and extensive fat marbling, including a 'fat-eye', which is deep fat. The meat is more tender than the sirloin steak because this part of the back (rib-eye) is slightly less muscular. Available with or without a bone (see Côte de boeuf). The relatively high fat percentage means that this meat has considerable flavor.

Côte de boeuf

The côte de boeuf is a rib-eye or sirloin steak attached to a rib bone with a layer of fat on the outside and clear fat marbling in the meat. Can also be served as spectacular prime rib, consisting of several ribs. See also prime rib.

OTHER NAMES:
TOP LOIN (SIRLOIN) STEAK,
NEW YORK STRIP (U.S.),
CONTREFILET (FRANCE)
PRICE: $ $ $
PLACE: SIRLOIN

OTHER NAMES:
DELMONICO STEAK (U.S.)
PRICE: $ $ $
PLACE: RIB

OTHER NAMES:
PRIME RIB, RIB-EYE STEAK,
COWBOY STEAK (U.S.),
COTE À L'OS (BELGIUM),
FINE RIB
PRICE: $ $ $
PLACE: RIB

Rib with rib-eye

Prime rib

The complete prime rib consists of 6 to 12 rib bones (counting from the head to the buttocks).

The meat is very soft and flavorful. If you want to make an impression on your butcher, ask for the first cut, which is rib 9 to rib 12, the part of the sirloin that contains the most subtle fat marbling. Anyone who loves marbled meat prefers the first section of the prime rib, ribs 6 to 10, which contains the rib-eye. The piece closer to the buttocks is smaller. Best when dry-aged on the bone. See also: Côte de boeuf.

Rump steak

Cut from the thick flank or from the topside, located around the buttocks of the animal. This is an eye of knuckle or topside knuckle. Knuckle from the thick flank is highly regarded by culinary purists because of its finer structure. The name is based on the shape of the part where rump steaks are cut from. The steak is very popular, lean, and fairly tender.

Dutch steak

This is a common term for any piece of steak that comes from the rump or topside, i.e. everything in and around the rear of the animal. The quality can vary greatly, from soft to quite tough, depending on the exact part cut. Lesser quality supermarket steak is 'tenderized' by pricking some short holes in the meat to penetrate the fibers. Dutch steak is a generic term used for steak that comes from Dutch cattle.

OTHER NAMES:
RIB ROAST (U.S.), FINE RIB
PRICE: $ $ $
PLACE: RIB

PRICE: $ $
PLACE: TOPSIDE/KNUCKLE

PRICE: $
PLACE: RUMP AND TOPSIDE

Porterhouse

T-bone

This is an impressive piece of steak, if only because of its size (14 ounces or more). The T-bone steak consists of the sirloin (the largest part) and the tenderloin (the small part). These two parts are separated by a T-shaped bone (lumbar vertebrae). The porterhouse steak is one variant of this popular American steak, which has the same shape, but contains a larger proportion of tenderloin because it is cut from a section that is further to the back. Lots of flavor, very tender and a favorite on the barbecue.

Brisket

The brisket is the most tender piece of meat from the shoulder and it is located on top of the shoulder blade. The fillet has the same shape as the tenderloin and it weighs between 10-28 ounces (depending on the size of the animal). This muscle has no function and is therefore super tender. The brisket is a cut of meat from the breast of the animal And it is very popular among Orthodox Jews as they are not allowed to eat meat that comes from the hindquarters. This is a good and cheap alternative to tenderloin (used for steak tartare for example).

Succade (peeled)

This part is normally used for pot roasts or beef roast. Ask your butcher to remove the tendon (hard piece of string) (called 'peeled' succade). This piece of meat does not normally look very attractive because it is coarsely chopped and it is not often displayed around the counter. The meat is very tasty, however, and has beautiful fat marbling, similar to the porterhouse steak. After peeling the average cattle produces less than 2 pounds of succade.

OTHER NAMES:
PORTERHOUSE
PRICE: $ $ $
PLACE: SIRLOIN

OTHER NAMES:
DIAMANTHAAS (BELGIUM)
PRICE: $ $
PLACE: SHOULDER

PRICE: $ $
PLACE: SHOULDER

Porterhouse

This type of steak is very popular in France and it comes from the muzzle (located next to the abdomen). This is work meat with a wonderful taste. Technically it is cut from the skirt and just like the thick skirt, this meat has a coarse, long thread. Butchers cut the meat diagonally against the grain, as you would carve salmon. The meat has a firm bite and it is full of flavor with a full, fatty taste provided by fat marbling.

Thick skirt

This meat is located in the chest near the tenderloin. Like the porterhouse this meat has a long and very coarse thread. This is a working muscle, which means that it is not very tender, but it is full of flavor. This is currently a very popular steak in trendy culinary circles. The thick skirt is usually cut in half along the length, which makes it easier to prepare. This is a very affordable piece of steak. Be careful not to overcook.

Shank steak

This is an unfashionable and undervalued piece from the hindquarters. A kind of Achilles tendon, just above the rear foot. It is very tender and very lean (no fat). Can also be prepared as a single roast in the oven.

PLACE: MUZZLE (ABDOMEN)
OTHER NAMES: SKIRT (U.S.)
PRICE: $

OTHER NAMES: ONGLET (FRANCE), HANGAR STEAK (U.S.), KRAAI (BELGIUM), BEENHOUWERS BIEFSTUK (NETHERLANDS), KARWEIVLEES (NETHERLANDS).
PLACE: CHEST
PRICE: $

OTHER NAMES: NONE
PLACE: SHANK
PRICE: $ $

Sirloin steak

From the thick rump of the animal. Extremely tender meat. Used to be called imitation beef fillet among butchers. Just a little more flavor than the tenderloin. Also suitable for cuts such as carpaccio.

Tail piece

Type of roast beef, but with more fat. Comes from a specific part of the buttock, known as the silverside. Suitable as a roast in the oven or as a steak in the pan. A tail piece steak has a similar rind of fat to sirloin. Some restaurants of ill repute sometimes sell tail piece, which is cheaper, as sirloin.

Wagyu

This is not a cut, but a type of steak that deserves to be mentioned separately. Wagyu beef is an exclusive breed of Japanese origin that is also bred outside of Japan these days. Wagyu beef contains high levels of fat marbling due to a special diet fed to the cattle before they are slaughtered, which gives the meat a unique taste. Many say that this is the best beef in the world. Wagyu is available in many different cuts (rib-eye, sirloin, porterhouse, etc.). Not all Wagyu is 100% pure.

PLACE: THICK RUMP
PRICE: $ $ $

OTHER NAMES: ROAST BEEF
PLACE: THICK RUMP AND TAIL PIECE
PRICE: $ $

PRICE: $ $ $ $ $

Messrs Vlot, father (right) and son,
own an independent butchery in
Brandwijk, in the Netherlands

A visit to an independent butcher

The independent butcher is a dying profession. Is there someone out there who wants to keep it going? Bert Vlot, an independent butcher in Randwijk, in the southern part of the Netherlands, is one of the few.

The Vlot family butchery V.O.F. is located along a main road in Randwijk, in the Netherlands. This is a traditional butchery, which has been owned by the same family since 1946. Bert (44) is currently the third generation butcher, who took over the company from his father Kees around 10 years ago. A crooked sign on the door states the opening hours: only open from Thursday to Saturday, from 8 a.m. "I am one of the last village butchers," said Bert with a grin. And indeed, you cannot help but wonder how a butcher can survive in such a desolate village, with major competition from the supermarket giants. But Bert knows better. Steak connoisseurs come from far and wide to his butchery to buy quality meat, including a growing group of South American expatriates who travel to Randwijk to buy picanha, which is a tail piece with extra fat that is very popular in Brazil. Another favorite is the exotic sounding costella minga, a kind of rib roast.

The reason for this is that Bert is one of the few independent butchers in the Netherlands with his own abattoir, which is a dying profession. It is estimated that there are only about 100 to 150 such butchers left in the country. You can ask for any special type of cut, and he will be able to give it to you.

In years gone by, it used to be normal for butchers to also slaughter the animals on their own. Butchers used to buy livestock at the cattle market where they haggled for the best price, after which the animals were slaughtered, boned and then sold from head to tail in their own butcheries. Scaling eventually left its mark on this industry too and these days the vast majority of butcheries in the Netherlands buy their meat wholesale, which is delivered in vacuum-packed plastic. This is certainly much easier and more efficient. The average butcher now spends more time on making displays more sophisticated than actually boning carcasses. When you ask for something that is a little bit different from the norm, chances are you will be faced with a blank stare. They only sell what they get. A rib-eye on the bone, you say? Hmm ... that could be a problem. But not for Bert Vlot. He knows his merchandise, inside and out. Literally.

Costs

Every week, small-scale farmers and livestock traders from the vicinity bring animals which are to be slaughtered to Bert's slaughterhouse, which is located at the back of the butchery. The area is covered with white tiles and there are saws, chains and meat hooks on the wall. 10 to 12 animals are slaughtered here every week. Two or three are destined for his own butchery, the rest for other ones, because it would be uneconomical to slaughter only for his own butchery. For this reason he also slaughters for farmers from the vicinity who consume the meat from their own animals, and also for a few livestock traders who sell the meat to wholesalers. Bert: "It cost me around Euro 400 just to pay the veterinarian and the grading master each time. I also need to invest in the slaughtering area to make sure that I comply with all of the rules. That means that it's simply not feasible to only slaughter one cow and a few pigs."

Escalating costs and ever increasing rules and regulations are the main reasons why there are hardly any small-scale slaughterhouses left in the Netherlands these days. It will certainly not make you rich. Independent butchers such as Bert are still active purely because they love their profession. Bert: "When I was still a young boy I started helping my grandfather to slaughter. When I turned eight I was allowed to cut the meat. I don't know anything else."

Slaughter

His father Kees (70) still helps him in the butchery and when we spoke to him he was busy working on Limousin beef, with a carcass hanging by its feet over a pot. "I've been doing this for more than 55 years," said Kees, using both arms in a well-practiced motion, as he cut away colossal organs and intestines, which then slipped from the rib cage into a container. Earlier the animal had been shot in the head with a captive bolt pistol so that it was brain-dead, after which its carotid artery was sliced in a single motion. There had been no roar or panic and everything was carried out calmly, even for the unsuspecting slaughter animal.

"Well built, not too big. It has fantastic hindquarters and a good meaty back," Bert said with satisfaction. The passport that came with the animal stated that it was born on 21/04/2009. Color: single color brown. Gender: female. Country of birth: Belgium. "I love young, female cattle," said Bert above the noise of electric saws and high pressure sprayers. "Two to three years old. The main growth period is then over and the meat is very tender. I love a fine thread, like a female Limousin or Piedmontese."

No additional meat

The cleaned carcasses are left to hang on a meat hook for at least one more day. After the carcass has been deboned and skinned it is divided into smaller parts and packed into vacuum bags to allow the meat to mature for at least one week. All of the meat sold in the shop was slaughtered on the premises, including beef, pork and lamb. All of the sausages are also home-made. When stock is depleted there is no more and no extra meat is bought from wholesalers.

This is also the reason the butchery is only open three days a week. When meat starts running out a sirloin steak can even end up in the meat grinder. Bert: "I am responsible for every pound of meat that goes out of those doors. Of course there is only one piece of the best meat available and in the past butchers used to save that for the mayor or for a good looking women that came into the shop. As a butcher you have to take care of what you sell your customers. When a Brazilian comes into my store and shows me a YouTube clip about a piece of meat that he's looking for, I will do my best to accommodate him. I think that's the beauty of meat: every culture has its own story when it comes to meat."

Kees, the father, took off his overalls and boots because his work was finished. He shook his head as he listened to the enthusiasm of his son. "I handed over my business to him about 10 years ago. Given another chance I probably wouldn't have done that, but what can you do, blood is thicker than water."

A visit to Nick Ottomanelli, a third-generation butcher from one of the most famous butcheries in New York: the Ottomanelli Brothers.

The butchery of the Ottomanelli Brothers is located in one of the most exclusive areas in New York, the Upper East Side. This is an old school butchery that is more than 100 years old, where they only sell prime quality meat. The floor is covered with sawdust, as used to be customary in every butchery, which is supposed to absorb blood from the carcasses when they are carried inside. A black-and-white portrait of grandfather Joseph Ottomanelli, who started the butchery in 1900 with his brother (initially only with a handcart), hangs on the wall.

The display cabinets are a carnivore's delight, packed with rib roasts, sirloin steaks and super-thick T-bone steaks, and all of it comes from organic farms in the region. There are also plenty of cowboy steaks available, which is a rib-eye with a bone, and which owes its name to the archetypal cowboys who used to grill this American cut over the open fire, while holding onto the bone with one hand. "Steaks from Ottomanelli are so tender you can eat them with a fork," they say in New York. It is very fashionable among New York foodies to be seen with a transparent shopping bag that contains a classic brown paper bag with the Ottomanelli logo on it.

Maturation

The 60-year-old Nick Ottomanelli, dressed in his indispensable white butcher's coat, currently runs the business with his brother Joey. They are the third-generation owners of the business. What is the secret of the perfect steak? "A steak must have a nice meaty flavor," said Nick. "With a crisp, dark crust and beautifully red on the inside." With a grin on his face he adds: "With a baked potato, a good salad and a nice bottle of red wine. And last but not least, a naughty girl. That's it! What more does a man need?"

Ottomanelli Bros.
Prime Meats & Poultry
Est. 1900
1549 York Avenue, New York, NY 10028
Tel: (212) 772-7900 · www.ottomanellibros.com
Fax: (212)-772-8436   DATE_____ 20___

8	Chicken Cutlets	43.90
6	N.Y. Strip	152.90
4	Porterhouse Steaks	126.40
6	Sweet Sausage	6.95

N° 863720

Ottomanelli specializes in so-called dry-aged beef, which is meat that has been matured for several weeks in special rooms where the humidity and the temperature are controlled. "Dry-aged is the best," said Nick. "The meat is the most tender and most flavorful meat you can imagine." In downtown Manhattan, in the Meatpacking District (formerly the beating heart of New York's meat industry, but today a collection of fashion boutiques and restaurants), Ottomanelli is one of the few remaining New York butchers that still has a warehouse where they mature meat. Every self-respecting steakhouse in New York now has dry-aged beef on the menu, often directly from the Ottomanelli's. How does Nick recognize a good quality piece of steak? "Beautiful marbling, evenly distributed over the steak. The color of the meat should be pink to deep red. And it must silky soft when you touch it."

meat that has been dry-aged is very expensive. Dry aging, which sometimes takes up to three or four weeks, is very expensive as the meat cannot be sold immediately. While maturing on the bone, the meat loses approximately 30% of its weight, which is a loss that butchers can only partially take into account. A nice dry-aged steak that has been matured for three weeks is much more expensive than a piece of meat that has not been matured. Nick's favorite cut? "The Porterhouse", he said firmly. "A nice thick eight ouncer on the bone, about 2 inches thick, enough for two people. Cooked medium rare." He prefers cooking his meat over a charcoal grill. His most important tip? Always use very coarse, freshly ground salt and pepper (Ottomanelli has its own line of salt and pepper). "Home, garden and kitchen salt is dust" does not sound like a compliment.

Supermarket

The meat from Ottomanelli is USDA Prime, the highest quality meat available according to the strict standards of the U.S. Department of Agriculture. Only one to two percent of the livestock qualifies to be certified as prime cut after it is slaughtered. Nick prefers the males from the Aberdeen Angus race. They are grass-fed and in the months prior to reaching the age at which they are ripe to be slaughtered, they are fed grains to develop extra fat. "We look very carefully when we select cattle," said the butcher. "Some bulls are fatter and more tender than others. Just like humans. I always want the fat ones. Not the overly active bulls, but the lazy ones, the slackers. They produce tender meat with the most beautiful fat and marbling." Americans prefer not to buy fat meat at supermarkets as consumers prefer lean meat. Many consumers think that fat is scary, and fatty

Tip from Nick: rest in the tent

What is the best way to let your steak rest? Never wrap it up completely in aluminum foil, warned Nick Ottomanelli. Otherwise, the meat will steam under the foil, which will compromise the crispy crust. Let the meat rest under a self-folded "tent" of aluminum foil, allowing the steam to escape through the ends.

OTTOMANELLI BROTHERS
1549 YORK AVENUE (CORNER OF 82ND STREET)
NEW YORK

STEAK

FROM FIELD TO TABLE

The Equipment

Techniques & Tools

Baking, frying, grilling, roasting, sous-vide or cooking at a low temperature in the oven? At any particular time, what is the best preparation technique? And what equipment is needed?

Heston Blumenthal, the world famous British chef and godfather of molecular gastronomy, wrote in his book *In Search of Perfection* about the quest to find out how to prepare the perfect steak. In the end he came up with a fascinating (and admittedly also a little time-consuming) combination of techniques. This method is based on slow cooking in the oven, at a very low temperature for a minimum period of 22 hours. The idea – which makes sense – is to prepare the meat at a low temperature, so that it does not dry out and maintains its juiciness and flavor. He takes a côte de boeuf (a single piece of approximately 2 pounds, with two bones) which he fries over a high heat with a super creme brulee burner, until the meat is brown on all sides. He then places the côte de boeuf in an oven at 122°F, and after 4 to 8 hours the core temperature will match this temperature ('a few degrees higher will ruin the recipe', the chef claims). The meat is then left in the oven at the same temperature for another 18 hours in order to tenderize the meat (type of dry aging). The meat is then removed from the oven and allowed two to four hours to reach room temperature. He then cuts the meat (vertically) into two pieces approximately 2 inches thick, each with a bone, and sprinkles coarsely ground sea salt and crushed peppercorns over the meat. The quirky chef finally fries the steaks in a red-hot iron frying pan with smoking peanut oil for 4 minutes on each side until brown, while he turns the steaks every 30 seconds. Blumenthal serves his perfect

steak with butter melted in a pan and Stilton cheese. In theory there's not much to argue about when it comes to this ingenious method, but it's not very practical, is it? Below is an overview of alternative techniques and tools for those who are also looking for a perfect result, but perhaps one that doesn't require quite so much work.

Grilling
Technique

Steaks with a rind of fat, such as sirloin steaks, are good for the grill because they remain nice and juicy. Always preheat the pan properly. Season the meat with salt and pepper. Place the meat on the frying pan. Optionally you can also rub some olive onto the meat well with a brush before putting it in the pan. The meat will initially stick to the pan, but it will eventually let go. Be careful not to turn the meat around too quickly. The steak can be grilled for a longer or shorter period of time, depending on the heat of the pan. For an extra juicy result you can also coat the meat with some extra olive oil while grilling.

TOOLS: Cast iron frying pan (without a vulnerable non-stick coat). A grill pan with high ridges is also very handy for making deep, sharp lines. This will also allow the fat to run away without coming into contact with the steaks. Clean the frying pan with light sandpaper and coat it with oil before putting it away. Also required: a brush to coat the meat.

BBQ
Technique

Grilling on the barbecue provides a lovely grilled flavor, which is excellent for T-bone steaks. Use charcoal or briquettes (they last longer), or a combination of the two. Make sure not to use firelighters with chemicals to start the fire as that could compromise the taste of the meat. Use a starter kit if necessary. Have patience: wait 30 to 40 minutes until the briquettes are covered with a thick gray layer of ash (braising heat) and with no more flames or embers visible.

Divide the smoldering charcoal into two layers of different heights to create grill zones with different temperatures. This is important when grilling T-bone steaks where the smaller part is tenderloin.
TOOLS: charcoal or gas barbecue.

Frying pan
Technique

Method: Preheat the frying pan for 2-3 minutes over a high heat. As soon as the pan is hot (check by letting a few drops of water fall into the pan – if the drops scatter and spatter the pan is hot enough), reduce the heat to medium. Put butter in the frying pan and let it bubble (the butter discolors and the foam pulls away). Steaks with more fat such as rib-eye or sirloin can also be cooked without any oil or butter (unless you want to make a gravy or sauce). Fry your steak on both sides until brown. First fry the side with the fat as that will provide the dripping with extra flavor. Reduce the heat when it looks like the steak and/or dripping could burn. Crucially: use the correct frying pan.

TOOLS: steel or stainless steel frying pan. A steel frying pan (an alloy of iron and some carbon) conducts heat well and it can become hot enough to sear the steak properly. Method: Burn-in the pan before using it for the first time. Cover the bottom with half a packet of salt and leave for 10 minutes on a high heat to clean the bottom (the pan may smoke). Throw the salt away. Pour oil into the pan and let it smoke for 10 minutes. The bottom will turn blue and clean. Maintenance: never wash the pan after use with water and detergent; instead wipe it clean with paper towels. Remember that iron can rust, so wipe the pan with a thin layer of oil before putting it away. After a few years of use the pan may turn black. If the pan does rust though, clean by frying salt and/or oil for 10 minutes at a high heat (or use a scouring pad).

Stainless steel pans consist of multiple layers and are made of stainless steel in combination with good heat conductors such as aluminum. These pans are resistant to high temperatures and conduct heat very well. The most conductive material is copper. Copper pans are (usually) lined with stainless steel to overcome the

Hot, hotter, hottest!

How do you know if your barbecue fire is hot enough? A simple test is to hold your hand about 4 inches above the heat and to count the seconds before it becomes too hot.

1-2 seconds – the coals are hot
3-4 seconds – the coals are medium hot
5-6 seconds – the coals are medium
6-7 seconds – the coals are medium cool
8-9 seconds – the coals are cool

If the fire is too hot, spread the charcoal over a larger area. If the fire is threatening to cool down, push the charcoal together and add more briquettes.

Broiler grill

A favorite at some of the better steak restaurants at home and abroad is the broiler grill. The steak is first preheated on an ordinary grill plate and then placed under the broiler for a few minutes. A professional high-tech (gas-fired) grill heats the steak at 2400 degrees Fahrenheit (!) from above. This professional super grills provide superior browning and crusting. The high temperature causes moisture to be released quickly, without the risk of overcooking the meat inside. You need to have your wits about you, however, because a steak can be charred quicker than you may think.

drawbacks of copper (copper can be harmful). These pans are quite pricey. Non-stick pans are not suitable for frying steaks as they are not very good at tolerating excessive heat. Also the pan does not create any encrustation at the bottom, which is used to make gravy. Note the size too. The butter (and the steak) burn faster in a pan that is too large. Ideally, leave a space of about a quarter of an inch between the steaks. An 11 inch frying pan is good for four large steaks. The 9 inch frying pan is good for two steaks, and for only one steak: 7 inches. A frying pan with an oven-proof handle (not plastic) is also very useful if you want to bake your steak in the oven for a bit. This is especially recommended for thick steaks such as filet mignon.

Oven
Technique
Suitable for large roasts such as roast beef, tail piece or rib roast. Method: first sear the meat in a frying pan, casserole or roasting pan. Use a pan that is large enough for the whole roast to fit in snug as the oil and fat burn faster in a pan that is too large. When the pan is too small the meat will end up boiling in its own dripping, which is not conducive to crust formation. Place the pan or roasting pan in a preheated oven. To keep the meat juicy, frequently baste while roasting with its own dripping, extra butter, broth or other moisture. If necessary, place a rack or grate at the bottom of the roasting pan to prevent the meat from simmering in its dripping. The cooking time depends on the tenderness of the meat (the more tender, the shorter the cooking time), whether it is with or without a bone (it takes longer with the bone), the thickness and whether you use a gas or hot air oven (hot air goes faster). It is easy to determine the doneness with a food probe. When the meat is raw you can first of all set the oven to a high temperature (480°F) until the meat is golden brown on the outside, then temper the temperature (350°F). This works especially well

Laguiole
pocket knife

It is easy to ruin a steak that has been prepared with the greatest care if you cut it with a blunt knife. Always make sure that you keep your knives razor-sharp. Always cut roasts with a long carving knife (also use a meat fork to hold the meat in place if necessary). A good knife has a long blade and is quite thin so you can cut very thin slices. Although tender steaks can be cut with the proverbial fork, you are in fact advised to always use sharp table knives. Do not use serrated knives, but rather knives with a smooth blade

(regularly sharpen the blades). Serrated steak knives – which are often provided in restaurants – cause a puddle of blood to come out of your steak. Laguiole pocket knives (pronounced: La-yol), named after the eponymous French village, are very good for this. Laguiole (population approximately 1,200) has dozens of workshops where these famous knives are made in the traditional manner. Some knives are made with wooden handles (forty different types of wood), while others are made from horn (cow or buffalo) or

bone. Each knife is made by hand and is unique. The makers carve their own decorations in the metal, by way of signature. Laguiole knives that were not manufactured in the village of the same name are also on the market, some of dubious quality (the name is not formally protected). An authentic Laguiole knife comes with a certificate and can easily cost more than $100 per knife. Some well known Laguiole workshops are Forge de Laguiole and Laguiole en Aubrac.

with roasts that are not easy to brown evenly in a pan because of an irregular shape or bone. Always allow the me to rest for at least 10 minutes before cutting the roast. Use a very sharp knife (!) to cut thin or thick slices, as desired.

TOOLS: gas oven or hot air oven. Also: roasting pan or oven-proof frying pan. Optional: roasting rack.

Sous-vide

Technique

With this method meat (or vegetables) is cooked in a hot water bath while vacuum-packed in plastic. Sous-vide cooking is usually done at low temperature (120 or 140°F). These mild temperatures ensure that the natural juices, vitamins, fragrances and tastes are better preserved and the meat becomes very tender. This method has become very popular among top chefs, partly because of the great accuracy it provides as food can be cooked until ready. To brown the steak, fry it briefly in a frying pan

after it has been prepared in a vacuum pack. Home varieties of professional Roner devices are also available at some of the better cooking utilities stores (available from about $400) which you can use to precisely cook a steak medium rare (126°F) in half an hour.

TOOLS: hot water bath (e.g. Sous Vide Supreme), vacuum device.

Raw

Technique

The most tender cuts of beef are great for raw preparations such as carpaccio or steak tartare. This includes beef tenderloin or a less common but also super tender part such as the brisket. Keep the meat and the kitchen equipment cool. Raw meat can quickly become ruined with heat. When preparing steak tartare, for instance, keep a second bowl ready with ice water to keep the finely chopped meat cool. Prepared raw meat preferably à la minute.

TOOLS: (optional) bowl with ice cubes.

How do I form diamond grill marks?

Use a grill pan with high ridges for a deep imprint. Sear the steak, placing it at an angle on the ridged surface. Give the steak a quarter turn and sear to form a diamond pattern. Turn the steak and do the same on the other side. Tip: when turning the steak, place it on a different part of the pan. As the previous part of the pan has been significantly cooled by the steak (the meat has removed heat from the pan), this will allow you to achieve better and more even browning. So it is better to use a large frying pan.

Cutting with the grain

If you look closely at your steak you will notice that fine, thin lines of muscle threads run through it. The more tender the meat, the finer the thread. Good tenderloin, for example, has very thin, barely visible threads. The longer and coarser the thread, the more chewy the meat. A good butcher cuts meat transversely (vertically) to the thread, cutting it in the middle, which makes the meat less chewy.

High or low temperature oven?

At a low temperature (below 260°F) meat will not dry out so quickly. Low temperatures are very suitable for tender meat that you also want to remain juicy. The cooking time is longer and there is not much browning. At a high temperature (390°F or more) meat turns brown faster and the outside is much hotter than the inside. There is also the risk of the meat cooking too rapidly and drying out. High temperatures are particularly suitable for smaller pieces of meat.

80

STEAK

FROM FIELD TO TABLE

Famous steaks

In French this is called filet de boeuf en croûte, while the British call this "compact tenderloin" Beef Wellington. This is an impressive dish that is excellent for serving at a dinner party, which also allows you to pay more attention to the side dishes while the meat is roasting in the oven.

PREPARATION: 1 HOUR
WAITING TIME: 30 MINUTES
OVEN TIME: 25 MINUTES

INGREDIENTS
SERVES 4

1 piece of tenderloin (20 ounces)
2 tablespoons Dijon mustard
1 pound mushrooms
5 ounces thinly sliced Parma ham
1 tablespoon flour
1 egg yolk, beaten
1 packet puff pastry, thawed

ALSO:
plastic film, basting brush,
shallow baking dish

TIP
Before baking, sprinkle coarse salt over the dough to make it look beautiful after baking.

1 *choose your meat*
Ask the butcher for a piece of even thickness to ensure that the tenderloin can cook evenly.

2 *browning*
Heat a frying pan over a high heat. Sprinkle the entire piece of meat with freshly ground salt and pepper. Turn the heat down a little when the pan is hot. Fry the tenderloin briefly over a medium heat. Let the tenderloin cool on a cutting board, then coat the meat with mustard.

3 *mushrooms*
Meanwhile, wipe the mushrooms clean and chop them finely with a knife (or use a food processor). Sprinkle with salt and pepper. Fry the mushrooms in a dry frying pan over a medium heat for 10-15 minutes until brown. Allow all the released moisture (a considerable amount!) to evaporate until you have a coarse, dry mushroom paste.

4 *roll*
Lay a large sheet of plastic wrap on the table with a square of Parma ham slices (a little overlap is okay). Spread the mushrooms evenly over the Parma ham, but leave about an inch free from the edges. Place the tenderloin in the middle and wrap the foil with Parma ham and mushroom paste tightly around the meat. Close off the ends of the foil and place in the refrigerator for at least half an hour.

5 *packet*
Preheat the oven to 350°F. On a table top dusted with flour, roll out the puff pastry into a $\frac{1}{10}$ inch thick square. Brush the edges with egg yolk. Brush the tenderloin lightly with egg yolk and put the meat in the middle of the dough. Cut away excess dough. Close the wrap and press the seams firmly. Place in the refrigerator for another five minutes.

6 *oven*
Brush the puff pastry all over with egg yolk. Make light, crosswise incisions (do not cut through the dough). Place the package on the seam in a shallow baking dish. Bake the Beef Wellington on a grill rack in the oven for about 25 minutes for medium-rare golden brown, and 5 minutes longer for medium.

7 *serve*
Put the Beef Wellington on a cutting board and cut the package in half. Cut the tenderloin into generous slices (1 inch thick) and serve on warm plates.

Harry's Bar carpaccio

1 *choose your meat*

Ask your butcher for an even piece around 2 ⅓ inches thick, cut from the thick center of the tenderloin.

2 *seasoning*

Coat the tenderloin (not the cutting surfaces) with mustard. Sprinkle the tenderloin with freshly ground salt and pepper. Sprinkle the seasoning on a plate. Roll the side of the meat with mustard firmly through the seasoning. Heat a bit of olive oil in a frying pan. Briefly brown the meat on the side with the seasoning. Let the meat rest for 5 minutes in aluminum foil.

3 *dressing*

Meanwhile, mix all of the ingredients together in a bowl and add salt and pepper to taste for a tangy sauce. Dilute with more cream if the dressing does not run off a spoon.

4 *flattening*

Slice the tenderloin with into four thin slices. Place two sheets of plastic wrap between each slice of meat. Carefully flatten the meat flat with a meat mallet or a heavy object, such as the bottom of a pan. Using a rolling pin, roll the meat out even more.

5 *serve*

Remove the top sheet of foil and turn over and place it on a plate. Remove the lower foil. Pour thin lines of dressing in a criss-cross pattern over the meat. Garnish with a tuft of salad rocket, capers and a quarter lemon. Sprinkle with freshly ground salt and pepper and optionally with a few parmesan shavings.

This is a simple recipe, but it is also easy to make mistakes when preparing this popular appetizer. Tip 1: Do not use meat that has been frozen and thawed. Tip 2: First round the tenderloin, before flattening the meat with a rolling pin. According to legend, carpaccio with a dressing was created in 1950 in Harry's Bar in Venice in 1950.

PREPARATION TIME: 30 MINUTES

INGREDIENTS
SERVES 4

1 piece of tenderloin (7 ounces)
1 tablespoon smooth mustard
2 tablespoons chopped herbs (e.g. rosemary, thyme, oregano)
1-2 tablespoons olive oil

FOR THE DRESSING
2 tablespoons extra virgin olive oil
1 tablespoon lemon juice
1 tablespoon grated horseradish (jar)
1 cap sour cream
2 tablespoons whipping cream

GARNISH
1 large handful salad rocket
2 tablespoons capers
1 lemon
optionally, a piece of parmesan cheese

ALSO:
aluminum foil, plastic wrap, rolling pin, a meat hammer (optionally)

According to culinary folklore, this piece of meat is named after the French writer and politician François René de Chateaubriand (1768-1848). This deliciously tender meat can be served with almost any steak sauce (such as Béarnaise or bordelaise).

1 *choose your meat*

Ask your butcher for top quality chateaubriand, which is normally cut from the top of the tenderloin, but can also be cut from the thick middle part of the tenderloin. Strictly speaking, a piece should weigh 13 ounces, but it is not a problem if it weighs slightly less or slightly more.

2 *browning*

Allow the meat time to reach room temperature. Preheat the oven to 210°F. Sprinkle the meat with coarsely ground salt and pepper. Heat an oven-proof frying pan over a high heat. Turn the heat down a little when the pan is hot. Melt a pat of butter, wait until the foam subsides and the butter starts to color. Brown the meat over a medium heat for 2-3 minutes on each side until golden brown.

3 *baking in the oven*

Remove the pan from the heat and insert a probe to the middle of the chateaubriand. Put the frying pan on a rack in the oven. Roast for about 25 minutes until the core temperature is 130°F for a medium-rare result. Shorter for rare (113°F), longer for medium (130°F – 140°F).

4 *rest*

Take the meat from the oven and let it rest on a baking rack for 10 to 15 minutes, loosely wrapped in a 'tunnel' of aluminum foil, with a plate for collecting liquids below.

5 *serve*

Cut the chateaubriand into ¾ inch thick slices and serve in warm plates.

PREPARATION TIME: 10 MINUTES
OVEN + RESTING TIME: 35 MINUTES

INGREDIENTS
SERVES 2

1 chateaubriand of 13 ounces
butter

ALSO:
probe, oven-proof frying pan,
aluminum foil

1 *choose your meat*

Côte de boeuf (also called côte à l'os) is ideal for maturing. Ask the butcher for a piece that has spent at least 3 weeks in a dry-age cell. Make sure that the meat is nicely veined, with a thick layer of fat for crackling on the outside.

2 *browning*

Give the meat time to reach room temperature. Preheat the oven to 210°F. Sprinkle the meat with coarsely ground salt and pepper. Heat an oven-proof frying pan over a high heat. Fry the côte de boeuf until golden brown. Peel and crush the garlic, and place it in the pan with the thyme sprigs. Sauté in the pan for 1-2 minutes to release the flavor.

3 *baking in the oven*

Remove the pan from the heat and let the meat rest for 5 minutes to cool. Put the pan with the contents in the oven. Insert a thermometer into the the center of the meat (not too close to the bone). Cees prefers rare meat where the core temperature should be 113°F, which takes about 20 minutes. For medium rare, it takes about 35 minutes (122 – 130°F) to cook the rib.

4 *edges*

Remove the pan with the côté de boeuf from the oven. Cut off the fat. Let the meat rest for 5-10 minutes, loosely wrapped in aluminum foil. Meanwhile, cut the fat into small pieces. Fry the crackling in the dripping from the meat.

5 *serve*

Cut the côté de boeuf into slices. Cut the last piece to the bone. Place the slices on a warm serving dish or plates. Sprinkle with a few spoons of meat dripping and sprinkle the crackling on top of that.

A firm part of the ribs, with beautiful fat marbling and a fatty edge. Served with the bone still attached and with crispy crackling. An all-time favorite which is a core recipe for three-star veteran Cees Helder.

PREPARATION TIME: 20 MINUTES
OVEN TIME: 20-35 MINUTES

INGREDIENTS
SERVES 2

1 piece of 30 ounces côté de boeuf,
with the bone
olive oil
3-4 cloves of garlic
3 stalks thyme

ALSO:
probe, oven-proof frying pan,
aluminum foil

Sirloin steak with Café de Paris butter

There's nothing much better than a soft melting pat of herb butter on a baked or grilled steak, so it's no wonder that Café de Paris has become such an integral part of French cuisine.

PREPARATION: 5 MINUTES
WAITING TIME: 30 MINUTES
PREPARATION TIME: 10 MINUTES

INGREDIENTS
SERVES 4

4 sirloins
FOR THE BUTTER
5 ounces farmers butter,
at room temperature
2 tablespoons ketchup
1 teaspoon Dijon mustard
½ teaspoon capers, chopped
1 teaspoon finely chopped chives
1 teaspoon chopped tarragon
2 anchovy fillets, chopped
1 teaspoon cognac
1 teaspoon Madeira wine (a fortified
Portuguese wine)
1 teaspoon Worcestershire sauce
1 pinch of paprika

ALSO:
grill pan, baking paper, aluminum foil

TIP
Variant: maître d'hotel-boter: mix
3 tablespoons chopped parsley, the
juice of ¼ lemon and a pinch of paprika
powder with 7 ounces soft butter.

1 *choose your meat*
Ask your butcher for sirloin with beautiful marbled fat (dry-aged) sirloins 1 ¾ inches thick and 8 ounces each.

2 *butter*
In a bowl, mix all the other ingredients together using a wooden spoon, then stir in the softened butter. Spoon the herb butter onto a piece of waxed paper or foil. Roll the butter up tightly and tie the ends shut. Place the butter roll in the refrigerator for at least 30 minutes.

3 *grilling*
Coat the sirloins with olive oil and sprinkle with freshly ground pepper and salt. Heat the grill pan over a high heat. Grill the sirloins for 1-2 minutes on each side for rare (3 minutes for medium-rare, 4 minutes for medium). Let the steaks rest for 5 minutes, loosely wrapped in aluminum foil.

4 *serve*
Cut the butter roll into ½ inch thick slices. Place the steaks on warm plates, with a slice of herb butter.

Sirloin steak with syrupy balsamic gravy

93

1 **choose your meat**
Ask your butcher for sirloins with beautiful marbled fat (dry-aged) 1 inch thick and 8 ounces each.

2 **bake**
Sprinkle the sirloin with coarsely ground salt and pepper. Heat a frying pan over a high heat. Turn the heat down a little when the pan is hot. Let a pat of butter melt, wait until the foam subsides and the butter starts to color. Grill the sirloins on a medium heat for 1-2 minutes on each side for rare (3 minutes for medium-rare, 4 minutes for medium). Reduce the heat when it looks like the butter might burn.

3 **the sauce**
Take 1 tablespoon dripping from the pan, drain the rest, then return the pan to a medium heat. Add the vinegar and scrape the encrustation from the pan using a wooden spoon. Allow the gravy to gently reduce for 5 to 10 minutes to a syrupy sauce. Add the thyme.

4 **serve**
Place the steaks on warm plates and spoon the balsamic gravy over them.

You don't need to buy traditional balsamic vinegar, which can be quite expensive, as you only need one drop for your steak. A cheaper version with a sprig of thyme from the garden should be enough to make a nice syrupy sauce in no time at all.

PREPARATION TIME: 25 MINUTES

INGREDIENTS
SERVES 4

4 sirloins
butter
5 fl oz balsamic vinegar
1 teaspoon fresh
thyme leaves, finely chopped

ALSO:
Aluminum foil

A South American classic sauce from Argentina. Good when prepared a few days earlier or perfect from the grill pan with a nice T-bone steak.

PREPARATION: 10 MINUTES

INGREDIENTS
SERVES 2

1 T-bone or porterhouse steak
(20 – 28 ounces)
olive oil

SAUCE
5 tablespoons finely chopped
flat-leaf parsley
4 cloves garlic, crushed
8 ½ fl oz extra virgin olive oil
½ cup red wine vinegar
2 tablespoons finely chopped red onion
1 teaspoon finely chopped
oregano (fresh or dried)
½ small red pepper, finely chopped

ALSO:
grill pan, basting brush, aluminum foil

1 *choose your meat*

Ask your butcher for a premium quality T-bone or porterhouse steak. If the look in his eyes is a look of incomprehension, try another butcher. A steak of 21-29 ounces (including the bone), 1 – 1 ½ inches thick, is more than enough for two people.

2 *salsa*

In a bowl, mix the parsley and the garlic pulp together, using a wooden spoon. Add the olive oil, vinegar and remaining ingredients and stir well. The chimichurri salsa should be nice and lumpy (thicker than vinaigrette). Let it stand for at least 30 minutes outside of the refrigerator to allow the flavor to develop. Properly sealed, the salsa can be kept in the fridge for a few days.

3 *grilling*

Give the steak time to reach room temperature. Brush the steak with olive oil and sprinkle with salt and pepper. Heat the grill pan over a high heat. Heat the grill pan over a high heat. Grill the steak for 3 minutes on each side for rare (4 minutes for medium-rare, 5 minutes for medium). Let the steak rest for 5 minutes, loosely wrapped in aluminum foil.

4 *serve*

Cut the meat from the bone, and into slices. Serve the steak on warm plates with the salsa on the side. Serve with crusty bread.

Steak with gravy and white bread à la Loetje

1 *choose your meat*
Ask your butcher for 4 thick slices of fillet steak. Preferably cut from the middle, 1 inch thick and 5-7 ounces each. Alternative: round steak (cheaper).

2 *bake*
Allow the meat time to reach room temperature. Sprinkle the steaks with coarsely ground salt and pepper. Heat a frying pan over a high heat. Turn the heat down a little when the pan is hot. Melt a pat of butter. Loetjes' butter trick: use lots of butter (a quarter of a pack per steak). Allow the butter to foam until the foam subsides and the butter starts to color. Grill the steaks on a medium heat for 1-2 minutes on each side for rare (3 minutes for medium-rare, 4 minutes for medium). Reduce the heat when it looks like the butter could burn. Loetje turns the steaks constantly (Jaap calls this 'dancing in the pan'). We prefer to leave them as they are, as that allows the steak to stay into contact with the frying pan, which results in better browning.

3 *rest*
Remove the steaks from the pan and let them rest for at least 5 minutes, loosely wrapped in a 'tunnel' of aluminum foil, on a grill with a plate for collecting liquids below. Meanwhile, make the gravy.

4 *gravy*
Return the pan to a medium heat and add a few tablespoons of hot water to cool the pan. The dripping will start to froth and partially vaporize. Scrape the encrustation from the pan using a wooden spoon. Let the gravy slowly reduce.

5 *serve*
Serve the steaks on warm plates, topped with lots of gravy. According to Jaap the steak must 'swim' in the gravy. Serve with slices of white bread and lettuce with vinaigrette.

Guests at Loetje café in the Amsterdam Concert Building often have to wait in line to enjoy the renowned steak with gravy from Loetjes. Owner Jaap Klinhamer disclosed his secret for this cookbook and the only change we made is that we replaced margarine, which he prefers, with butter, but we stuck with his preference of white bread and gravy in abundance.

PREPARATION TIME: 10 MINUTES

INGREDIENTS
SERVES 4

4 fillet steaks
1 crispy fresh white bread
creamy butter (not margarine)

ALSO:
Aluminum foil

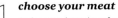

With a handful of fresh seaasonal mushrooms, a dash of whiskey and some whipped cream you can quickly make a wonderful sauce that bursts with flavor.

PREPARATION TIME: 20 MINUTES

INGREDIENTS
SERVES 4

4 steaks
7 ounces (mixed) mushrooms
(e.g. chanterelles, button mushrooms, shiitake)
creamy butter
5 fl oz veal stock (jar)
¾ cup whipping cream
1 tablespoon whiskey
1 lime

ALSO:
Aluminum foil

1 *choose your meat*

Ask your butcher for rump steak (or sirloin steak), preferably cut from the middle, 1 inch thick and 5-7 ounces each. This sauce is also excellent with grilled rib-eye steak or a thick sirloin.

2 *sauce*

Cut or break the stems from larger mushrooms, if that's what you are using. Leave a few smaller mushrooms aside to use later as garnish. Wipe them clean with a brush or a bit of kitchen paper. Do not rinse with water. Heat a little butter in a pan and sauté the mushrooms over a medium heat until brown. Remove from the pan and set aside. Add the meat stock, cream and whiskey and stir well. Let the sauce reduce for about 20 minutes until only one-third remains. Add the fried mushroom pieces (remember to keep some aside for garnish) and stir into the sauce. Keep the sauce warm.

3 *bake*

Allow the meat time to reach room temperature. Sprinkle the steaks with coarsely ground salt and pepper. Heat a frying pan over a high heat. Turn the heat down a little when the pan is hot. Let melt a pat of butter, wait until the foam subsides and the butter starts to color. Fry the steak on a medium heat for 1-2 minutes on each side for rare (3 minutes for medium-rare, 4 minutes for medium). Reduce the heat when it looks like the butter could burn.

4 *rest*

Let the steak rest for 5 minutes, loosely wrapped in aluminum foil. Meanwhile, freshen the sauce up with freshly squeezed lime juice.

5 *serve*

Serve the steaks on warm plates, topped with lots of gravy. Garnish with a few small mushrooms.

1 choose your meat
Ask your butcher for 4 thick slices from the middle of the fillet, 1 – 1 ½ inches thick and 5-7 ounces each.

2 wine reduction
In a frying pan, melt some butter over a low heat. Gently fry the carrot, shallot, mushrooms, bay leaf and parsley for 3-4 minutes. Add the wine and allow it to reduce for 10-15 minutes to 3 ¼ fl oz. Note that the wine should not boil, just steam. Strain the wine. Set the shallots aside and dispose of the remaining vegetables. Pour the wine back into the frying pan and reduce over a low heat for 15-20 minutes until only 2 tablespoons remain. Keep aside in a bowl.

3 bake
Allow the meat time to reach room temperature. Sprinkle the tenderloin with coarsely ground salt and pepper. Heat a frying pan over a high heat. Turn the heat down somewhat when the pan is hot. Melt a pat of butter, wait until the foam subsides and the butter starts to color. Fry the steak on a medium heat for 1-2 minutes on each side for rare (3 minutes for medium-rare, 4 minutes for medium). Reduce the heat when it looks like the butter could burn.

4 rest
Let the tenderloin rest for 5 minutes, loosely wrapped in aluminum foil. Meanwhile make the sauce.

5 sauce
Take 1 tablespoon dripping from the pan, drain the rest, then return the pan to a medium heat. Sauté the shallots for 1-2 minutes until soft. Add the broth and scrape the encrustation from the pan using a wooden spoon. Let the sauce reduce for about 10 minutes until only 4 tablespoons remain. Add the reduced wine to the dripping released while the meat was resting. With a whisk, beat the lumps of cold butter one by one into the sauce. Add a new lump of butter only when the previous one has been properly melted. The sauce should be thick and glossy. Stir in the shallots and thyme. Season to taste with salt and pepper.

6 serve
Serve the tenderloin on warm plates, topped with a spoon of gravy. Serve with crusty bread.

A steak for a true meat lover. A delicate piece of meat, very tender with subtle flavor. Served with bordelaise sauce, a powerful red wine sauce with a shallot flavor. You don't need to use your most expensive bottle of wine, but make sure not to use the cheapest stuff you can find either.

PREPARATION: 40 MINUTES
COOKING TIME: 15 MINUTES

INGREDIENTS
SERVES 4

4 pieces tenderloin steak
butter
for the wine reduction
1 small carrot, chopped
4 small shallots, peeled
4 mushrooms, chopped
1 bay leaf
3 sprigs parsley
8 ½ fl oz red wine

SAUCE
2 shallots, finely chopped
8 ½ fl oz beef or chicken broth
1 ¾ ounces ice-cold, unsalted butter, cut into lumps
1 teaspoon fresh thyme leaves

ALSO:
conical strainer, aluminum foil

Sour cream Béarnaise sauce goes well with any piece of steak. Here it is served with the steak of all steaks: rib-eye.

PREPARATION: 20 MINUTES
COOKING TIME: 10 MINUTES

INGREDIENTS
SERVES 4

4 rib-eye steaks
butter

SAUCE:
4 sprigs of fresh tarragon
2 tablespoons white wine vinegar
1 teaspoon black or
white peppercorns, crushed
1 small shallot, finely chopped
9 ounces of butter
2 egg yolks
juice of ½ lemon
pinch of cayenne pepper
1 tablespoon finely chopped chervil

ALSO:
conical strainer, aluminum foil

TIP
It is faster with a blender: beat the yolks in the blender for 1 minute. Add the boiled liquid. Add the melted butter in a thin stream. Mix the herbs and season to taste.

1 **choose your meat**
Ask your butcher for beautiful marbled fat (dry-aged) rib-eye steaks, 1 ¾ inches thick and 8 ounces each.

2 **sauce**
Pick the tarragon leaves from the stems, and separately chop both fine. Mix the vinegar with 2 tablespoons water, tarragon stems, peppercorns and shallot shreds in a saucepan. Simmer over a low heat for 5-10 minutes until reduced by half. Strain the liquid over another saucepan. Wipe the pan clean and melt the butter in it over a low heat, without browning. Beat the yolks through the reduced vinegar. Put the pan over a low heat on the smallest burner – use a flame distributor if necessary. Beat with a whisk for at least 5 minutes, until the mixture starts to bind. Add the melted butter in a thin stream while stirring. The sauce should be lumpy and run from the whisk like a string. Season with lemon juice, salt and cayenne pepper. Stir in the tarragon and chervil. Keep the sauce warm. In a bain-marie (saucepan in a larger pan with boiling water) or in a clean thermos (without any odor!).

3 **bake**
Allow the meat time to reach room temperature. Sprinkle the rib-eye steaks with coarsely ground salt and pepper. Heat a frying pan over a high heat. Turn the heat down somewhat when the pan is hot. A good rib-eye has enough fat and can be baked fine without any butter. Otherwise, melt a pat of butter, wait until the foam subsides and the butter starts to color. Fry the steak on a medium heat for 1-2 minutes on each side for rare (4 minutes for medium-rare, 5 minutes for medium). Do not move the steaks while baking. Reduce the heat when it looks like the butter could burn.

4 **rest**
Let the steak rest for 5 minutes, loosely wrapped in aluminum foil.

5 **serve**
Serve the rib-eye steaks on warm plates, topped with a spoon of lukewarm gravy.

Rib-eye with a shallot & butter sauce

1 choose your meat

Ask your butcher for beautiful marbled fat (dry-aged) rib-eye steaks, 1 ¾ inches thick and 8 ounces each.

2 bake

Allow the meat time to reach room temperature. Sprinkle the rib-eye steaks with coarsely ground salt and pepper. Heat a frying pan over a high heat. Turn the heat down a little when the pan is hot. A good rib-eye has enough fat and can be baked fine without any butter. Otherwise, melt a pat of butter, wait until the foam subsides and the butter starts to color. Fry the steak on a medium heat for 1-2 minutes on each side for rare (4 minutes for medium-rare, 5 minutes for medium). Do not move the steaks while baking. Reduce the heat when it looks like the butter could burn.

3 rest

Let the steak rest for 5 minutes, loosely wrapped in aluminum foil. Meanwhile make the sauce.

4 sauce

Take 1 tablespoon dripping from the pan, drain the rest, then return the pan to a medium heat. Sauté the shallots for 1-2 minutes until soft. Add the broth and scrape the encrustation from the pan using a wooden spoon. Let the sauce reduce for about 10 minutes until only 4 tablespoons remain. Add the dripping released while the meat rested. With a whisk, beat one spoon of cold butter into the sauce. Add a new lump of butter only when the previous one has been properly melted. The sauce should be thick and glossy. Mix the parsley in. Season to taste with salt, pepper, lemon juice and optionally with some fresh thyme leaves.

5 serve

Serve the rib-eye steaks on warm plates, topped with a spoon of gravy.

A fantastic and very easy sauce that goes well with any steak. Ideal if you have limited time and you do not want to put "bare" meat on the table. Good match with a juicy rib-eye.

COOKING TIME: 15 MINUTES

INGREDIENTS
SERVES 4

4 rib-eye steaks
butter

SAUCE
2 small shallots, finely chopped
8 ½ fl oz beef or chicken broth
4 tablespoons ice-cold, unsalted butter
1 tablespoon finely chopped parsley
1 teaspoon lemon
thyme (optional)

ALSO:
conical strainer, aluminum foil

A real treat for any carnivore is the prime rib. Juicy from the melted fat, red-pink on the inside and with a golden-brown, crispy crust is the perfect way to serve it. Mistakes in the preparation of this meat can normally be traced back to the oven.

COOKING TIME: 20 MINUTES
OVEN TIME: 20-35 MINUTES

INGREDIENTS
SERVES 4

1 prime rib of 4 ½ pounds
butter
4 cloves garlic
4 stalks thyme

ALSO:
probe, oven-proof
frying pan, aluminum foil

1 *choose your meat*

Ask your butcher to cut a rib-eye with 4 beautifully cut and clean bones. The rib consists of seven ribs, i.e. ribs 6 to 12. If you want to get the very best (and impress your butcher), ask for the section between ribs 9 and 12, which is also known as the first cut or prime rib. This is the sirloin. The rib-eye is located in another section, closer to the shoulder.

2 *browning*

Allow the meat time to reach room temperature. Sprinkle the meat with coarsely ground salt and pepper. Preheat the oven to 355°F. Preheat an oven-proof frying pan. Turn the heat down slightly and melt a pat of butter. Brown the ribs on all sides over a medium heat. First fry the fatty side, which provides the dripping with extra flavor. Peel and crush the garlic, and place it in the pan with the thyme sprigs. Sauté in the pan for 1-2 minutes to release the flavor.

3 *baking in the oven*

Remove the pan from the heat and let the meat rest for 5 minutes to cool. Put the pan with the contents in the oven. Insert a thermometer into the the center of the meat (not too close to the bone). After about 20 minutes, at a core temperature of 113°F, the meat is still pretty raw. which takes about 20 minutes. For medium rare, it takes about 35 minutes (122 – 130°F) to cook the rib. Please note that the meat will become a few degrees warmer still when you let it rest.

4 *rest*

Leave the roast to rest in the oven for 5-10 minutes. Loosely wrap in aluminum foil, or turn the oven off with the door open.

5 *serve*

Cut the ribs on a cutting board using a razor-sharp carving knife into ¼ inch slices, or thicker if you prefer. Cut the last piece to the bone. Serve each person 3 or 4 slices of meat on warm plates, with a gravy or herb butter.

1 choose your meat
Ask your butcher for a tail piece with the layer of fat still attached as it keeps the meat tender and provides more taste. The meat is naturally at its best when dry-aged for a few weeks.

2 browning
Allow the meat time to reach room temperature. Preheat the oven to 250°F. Sprinkle the tail piece with freshly ground salt and pepper. Preheat an oven-proof frying pan. Place the meat with the fatty layer down, fry for 2-3 minutes over a medium heat until the fat has melted. Now roast the meat until golden brown.

3 baking in the oven
Place the tail piece in an oven pan or place the pan, contents and all, on a roasting rack in the middle of the oven. Bake in the oven for 35 minutes for rare and 45 minutes for medium. Use a probe (rare 113°F, medium-rare 130°F, medium 130°F – 140°F).

4 sauce
In a saucepan, mix the red wine broth, shallot slices, thyme sprigs and half of the blueberries together. Bring to a boil, then reduce the heat. Reduce the sauce for about 10 minutes until only half remains; cook the blueberries whole. Strain the sauce over a bowl.

5 rest
Leave the roast to rest in the oven for 5-10 minutes. Loosely wrap in aluminum foil, or turn the oven off with the door open. Meanwhile make the sauce. Pour the sauce and the dripping from the baking dish into a saucepan. Add the remaining blueberries and heat over a medium heat until the berries start to burst.

6 serve
Cut the tail piece into thin slices. Serve the slices on warm plates, topped with a spoon of gravy. Serve with oven-roasted potatoes.

The tail piece – not to be confused with the oxtail – is a less commonly used piece of meat under the thick loin, which is an extension of the silverside. It may be cheaper, but in many ways it is equal to roast beef and it can be served with a blueberry sauce, which is easy to make.

COOKING TIME: 30 MINUTES
OVEN TIME: 35-45 MINUTES

INGREDIENTS
SERVES 4

1 small tail piece or part of a tail piece
of just over 2 pounds
15 fl oz red wine
10 fl oz beef broth
4 shallots, finely chopped
2 stalks thyme
9 ounces blueberries

ALSO:
plastic foil, basting brush, shallow strainer,
aluminum foil, food probe (optional)

The spectacular Bistecca alla Fiorentina combines the best of both worlds: the sirloin and the tenderloin. Roasted over a charcoal fire for that characteristic barbecue flavor with a nice brown, handsome crust is much better than baked in the pan.

PREPARATION: 40 MINUTES
COOKING TIME: 15 MINUTES

INGREDIENTS
SERVES 2

1 T-bone or porterhouse steak
(20 – 28 ounces)
extra virgin olive oil
1 lemon, quartered

ALSO:
barbecue with charcoal and
a clean grill, aluminum foil

TIP
Rub the steak in advance with a halved garlic clove (some purists consider this to be a mortal sin).

1 *choose your meat*
Ask your butcher for a steak of 20 – 28 ounces (including the bone), 1 – 1 ½ inches thick, which should be more than enough for two people.

2 *barbecue*
Fire up the barbecue and wait until a thin layer of gray ash has formed around the coals, which should take about 30 minutes. Stack some of the hot coals in layers on the one side, and on the other side distribute the rest of the charcoal in a single layer over the surface of the barbecue. You will create two heat zones in this manner. Check: if you can keep your hands at a distance of 5 inches above the barbecue grill for 3 to 4 seconds, the coals are medium-hot. The other side must be medium low, where you should be able to hold your hand for seven seconds.

3 *grilling*
Allow the steak time to reach room temperature. Brush the steak with olive oil and sprinkle with salt and pepper. Put the T-bone steak on the grid so that the tenderloin portion is above the cooler charcoal fire and the sirloin steak over the hot side. Grill the steak for 2-3 minutes or until golden brown on each side. Then cook the steak over the cooler section: 3 to 4 minutes for rare, 5-6 minutes for medium-rare, 7-8 minutes for medium. Turn occasionally. Also grill the lemon for the last minute. Let the steak rest for 5 minutes, loosely wrapped in aluminum foil.

4 *serve*
Cut the meat from the bone, and into slices. Serve the steak on warm plates. Drizzle with olive oil and a pinch of lemon.

Steak au poivre with peppercorn cream sauce

1 *choose your meat*

Ask your butcher for beautiful marbled fat (dry-aged) sirloins, 1 ¾ inches thick and 8 ounces each.

2 *sauce base*

Over a medium heat, melt 1 tablespoon butter in a frying pan. Fry the shallot shreds for 1-2 minutes. Add the broth and bring to a boil over a high heat. Allow the liquid to reduce to half a cup in 10 minutes. Strain the broth over a bowl.

3 *peppercorns*

Meanwhile, crush the peppercorns with the rolling pin or with the bottom of a heavy pan, but make sure not to crush them too fine. It helps to place the peppercorns in a plastic bag or to fold them in a towel before crushing them. Sprinkle the sirloins with salt. Rub the top of each steak firmly with 1 teaspoon crushed peppercorns.

4 *baking*

Heat the frying pan over a high heat. Turn the heat down a little when the pan is hot. Put the sirloins, without butter or oil, with the side with the peppercorns facing up. While cooking, apply pressure on the meat, with a heavy frying pan for instance, so that the peppercorns can attach

properly to the meat. Cook the sirloins over a medium heat for 3 minutes on each side for medium-rare (or for more or less time as preferred). Let the steaks rest for 5 minutes, loosely wrapped in aluminum foil.

5 *sauce*

Take 1 tablespoon dripping from the pan, drain the rest, then return the pan to a medium heat. Add the shallot broth from step 1, the cream and 3 tablespoons cognac. Scrape the encrustation from the pan using a wooden spoon. Allow the sauce to simmer for 5 minutes while continuously stirring. Beat in the lemon juice, a tablespoon cognac and the rest of the dripping. With a whisk, beat one tablespoon of cold butter into the sauce. Add a new lump of butter only when the previous one has been properly melted. The sauce should be thick and glossy.

6 *serve*

Serve the steak au poivre on warm plates and spoon the pepper sauce over the meat. Serve with crusty bread.

A brasserie classic, which also has a few variations (some more successful than others). Sometimes served only with crushed peppercorns, but we prefer the version with a peppery cream sauce.

PREPARATION: 15 MINUTES
COOKING TIME: 10 MINUTES

INGREDIENTS
SERVES 4

4 sirloins
4 teaspoons black peppercorns

SAUCE
4 tablespoons ice cold unsalted butter
1 shallot, finely chopped
8 ½ fl oz beef broth
5 fl oz chicken broth
3 tablespoons whipping cream
3 tablespoons + 1 tablespoon cognac
1 teaspoon lemon juice

ALSO:
aluminum foil, conical strainer

In Italy steak is nearly always served with a tomato sauce, with a hint of a good pizza sauce, and *aglio e peperoncino* (lots of garlic and pepper) makes it a little spicy. Preferably sirloin must be used, but knuckle beef, which is slightly less expensive, can also be used.

COOKING TIME: 25 MINUTES

INGREDIENTS
SERVES 4

4 sirloins
1 tablespoon olive oil

SAUCE
1 can peeled tomatoes (14 ounces)
2 teaspoons extra virgin olive oil
1 small onion, finely chopped
1 red pepper, finely chopped
5 cloves garlic, crushed
1 tablespoon tomato paste
3 tbsp red wine
1 sprig of oregano
3 tablespoons finely chopped parsley

ALSO:
blender or food processor,
aluminum foil

1 *choose your meat*
Ask your butcher for fairly thin sirloins with beautiful fat marbling (dry-aged), ¾ inch thick and 5-7 ounces each.

2 *preparation*
Preheat the oven to 300°F. Allow the meat time to reach room temperature. Sprinkle the sirloins with coarsely ground salt and pepper. Puree the contents of the canned tomatoes with a hand blender or in a food processor.

3 *bake*
Heat a frying pan over a high heat. Turn the heat down a little when the pan is hot. Pour the olive oil into the pan, wait until the oil begins to smoke. Grill the sirloins on a medium heat for 1-2 minutes on each side for rare (3 minutes for medium-rare, 4 minutes for medium). Let the steaks rest for 5 minutes, loosely wrapped in aluminum foil.

4 *sauce*
Take 1 tablespoon dripping from the pan, drain the rest, then return the pan to a medium heat. Sauté the onion for 2-3 minutes. Stir in the red pepper, garlic and tomato puree. Simmer for one minute. Pour the wine and tomato puree into the pan and add a sprig of oregano. Scrape the encrustation from the pan using a wooden spoon. Add the dripping released while the meat was resting. Allow the sauce to simmer for 5 minutes while continuously stirring.

5 *serve*
Serve the steaks on warm plates, spoon the tomato sauce over them and sprinkle with parsley. Serve with ciabatta and a rocket salad.

1 choose your meat

Ask your butcher for brisket, which is also the meat they use at Flo. This meat has more flavor and it's also cheaper than tenderloin. You may have to order the meat in advance, or otherwise ask for the most succulent tenderloin steak or the best knuckle beef that the butcher has.

2 cut

Cut the meat into strips and chop it into tiny cubes, but not too fine (¼ x ¼ inch) – the steak tartare should still have some bite. Use a sharp knife, otherwise you will destroy the steak. Keep the meat cool in a glass bowl on ice (preferably in a second bowl). It is possible to cut the meat a few hours in advance, but make sure to keep it properly covered (on ice) in the refrigerator.

3 dressing

Using a fork, whisk the yolks and the mustard together in a bowl. Add Worcestershire sauce, Tabasco, salt and pepper to taste. Add an equal volume of olive oil to the egg yolk mixture, drop by drop. Slice the shallot, parsley, capers and pickles very fine. Fold it through the yolk mixture.

4 finish

Just before serving, stir the chopped beef through the dressing. Season with more Tabasco, salt or freshly ground pepper, if preferred.

5 serve

Spoon the steak tartare in a circular shape, 1 ¾ inches thick (the size of a burger patty) onto chilled plates. Using a for, draw a few lines through the top of the meat. Season with more pepper.

Steak tartare is surprisingly simple to prepare. Success factor 1: buy the right steak (e.g. brisket). Success factor 2: add the right seasoning. Success factor 3: use your hands, do not chop the meat in a food processor. This recipe came from Rudolph Forest, the head chef at Flo Amsterdam.

PREPARATION TIME: 25 MINUTES

INGREDIENTS
SERVES 4

21 ounce brisket
4 egg yolks
4 teaspoons mustard
olive oil
Worcestershire sauce
Tabasco
1 shallot, peeled
½ bunch parsley
1 tablespoon capers
2 ounces cornichons (crunchy, sour pickles)

ALSO:
bowl of ice cubes

TIP
Steak tartare is often presented in restaurants with the additional ingredients on the side. It is your decision if you want to mix the ingredients in yourself, or if you want that to be done in the kitchen. Opt for the latter, because you will never be able to mix it properly on your plate.

Piccalilli is easy to make yourself and delicious. It is also underrated and it tends to be left out when seasoning red meat. This recipe comes from one of my favorite steak restaurants in Belgium: Saint Cornil in Aalbeke (Kortrijk). The meat used in this recipe is not their famous côte à l'os, but rather the trusty old brisket. Start to make the sauce at least one day in advance!

PREPARATION: 15 MINUTES
WAITING TIME: 1 DAY + 40 MINUTES
PREPARATION TIME: 10 MINUTES

INGREDIENTS
SERVES 4

21 ounce brisket
butter

SAUCE
12 fresh pearl onions
1 head cauliflower, cut into small florets
2 large cucumbers, sliced
20 fl oz white wine vinegar
10 fl oz malt vinegar (a little sweeter than ordinary vinegar, normally used in England with fish & chips)
½ teaspoon red pepper, finely chopped
10 ounces caster sugar
3 tablespoons mustard powder
1 ½ tablespoons turmeric
4 tablespoons cornstarch

ALSO:
conical strainer, clean bottle with a screw cap, oven-proof frying pan, probe, aluminum foil

1 *choose your meat*
Ask your butcher for one piece of brisket, or alternatively ask for two smaller fillets.

2 *one day in advance*
Cook the pearl onions for 2 minutes in salted water. Rinse them in a strainer under cold running water to make the peeling easier, as the onions will then simply fall from the peel. Mix the pearl onions in a bowl with the cauliflower and pickles. Soak the vegetables for the night in a bowl filled with water and a pinch of salt (the vegetables should only just be covered with water). In a saucepan, bring both types of vinegar and the red pepper to a boil. Make sure to switch on the extractor fan to get rid of the acidic vapors. Let it reduce for 3 to 4 minutes, then pour the vinegar into a bowl through a strainer. Set aside.

3 *piccalilli*
In a large bowl, mix the sugar, mustard powder, turmeric and cornstarch with a few teaspoons of cold vinegar to form a smooth paste. Bring the remaining vinegar to a boil. Whisk the vinegar into the mustard paste and pour the mixture back into the steel pan. Let the sauce bind for 3 minutes over a medium heat. Strain the vegetables. Scoop them into a bowl with the warm sauce. After it has cooled down, place the piccalilli in a sealed jar, which can be kept in the refrigerator for up to one month.

4 *sear*
Allow the meat time to reach room temperature. Preheat the oven to 320°F. Sprinkle the meat with coarsely ground salt and pepper. Heat an oven-proof frying pan over a high heat. Turn the heat down a little when the pan is hot. Melt a pat of butter, wait until the foam subsides and the butter starts to color. Fry the brisket over a medium heat until golden brown.

5 *baking in the oven*
Remove the pan from the heat and insert a probe to the middle of the meat. Put the frying pan on a rack in the oven. Roast for about 25 minutes until the core temperature is 130°F for a medium-rare result. Less for rare (113°F), more for medium (130°F – 140°F).

6 *rest*
Take the meat from the oven and let it rest on a baking rack for 10 to 15 minutes, loosely wrapped in a 'tunnel' of aluminum foil, with a plate for collecting liquids below.

7 *serve*
Cut the meat into slices ¾ – 1 inch thick and serve on a warm plate with the piccalilli on the side.

Steak sandwich with creamy mustard mayonnaise

1 choose your meat
Ask your butcher to cut you eight thin slices of rump steak, or cut the meat yourself. You can also use a small steak with a rim of fat, such as sirloin or rib-eye. Place two sheets of plastic wrap between each slice of meat. Carefully flatten the meat flat with a meat mallet or a heavy object, such as the bottom of a pan, until about ⅓ inch thick.

2 sauce
In a bowl, mix the mayonnaise with the mustard. Stir in the gherkins and capers. Season with freshly ground pepper, salt and lemon juice.

3 grilling
Allow the meat time to reach room temperature. Preheat the oven to 390°F. Coat the slices of meat with olive oil and sprinkle with freshly ground pepper. Heat the grill pan over a high heat. Grill the thin meat slices in 2 portions, 1 minute on each side for medium-rare, slightly longer for medium. Let the meat rest for 5 minutes, loosely wrapped in aluminum foil.

4 buns
Meanwhile, bake the buns for a few minutes in the preheated oven until hot and crispy. Cut the buns in half and allow all the steam to escape.

5 serve
Spread the halves of the rolls with the mustard and mayonnaise mix. Place the steaks on the bottom half of the buns and garnish with a tuft of salad rocket. Place the top half of the bun on top and press down firmly.

A sandwich with a perfectly grilled thin steak can be made in a jiffy. Juicy, crunchy, creamy and fresh at the same time – a perfect lunchtime snack! Also ideal for a light evening meal.

PREPARATION TIME: 15 MINUTES

INGREDIENTS
SERVES 4

21 ounce rump steak, single piece
olive oil
4 buns, e.g. ciabatta
salad rocket (or lettuce)

SAUCE
3 tablespoons mayonnaise
1 tablespoon Dijon mustard
1 tablespoon finely chopped cornichons
(crunchy, sour pickles)
1 tablespoon finely chopped capers
juice of ½ lemon

ALSO:
plastic wrap, meat hammer,
grill pan, aluminum foil

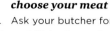

A French bistro classic that you simply have to try. Do not compromise on the quality of the foie gras and truffle. You can also replace the foie gras with chicken liver pâté.

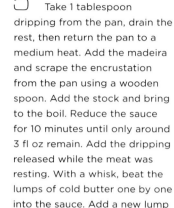

PREPARATION TIME: 45 MINUTES

INGREDIENTS
SERVES 4

4 small pieces filet mignon
butter for frying

SAUCE
4 tablespoons madeira (or port)
13 fl oz veal or beef stock (canned)
1 ¾ ounces ice-cold, unsalted
butter, cut into lumps

SIDE DISH
4 thick slices white bread,
without crusts
4 slices of foie gras
(size of the filet mignon)
1 ½ ounces fresh black truffle

ALSO:
cutter or glass (size of the filet mignon),
aluminum foil, truffle slicer or mandolin

1 *choose your meat*
Ask your butcher for even slices of filet mignon: 1 – 1 ½ inches thick and 5-6 pounds each. Allow the meat time to reach room temperature.

2 *toast*
Cut circles from the white bread and toast them until crisp and golden brown in a toaster (or under the oven grill).

3 *bake*
Meanwhile, sprinkle the filet mignon with coarsely ground salt and pepper. Heat a frying pan over a high heat. Turn the heat down a little when the pan is hot. Melt a pat of butter, wait until the foam subsides and the butter starts to color. Grill the filet mignon on a medium heat for 3 minutes on each side for rare (5 minutes for medium-rare, 7 minutes for medium). Reduce the heat when it looks like the butter could burn.

4 *rest*
Take the meat from the oven and let it rest on a baking rack for 10 to 15 minutes, loosely wrapped in a 'tunnel' of aluminum foil, with a plate for collecting liquids below. Meanwhile make the sauce.

5 *sauce*
Take 1 tablespoon dripping from the pan, drain the rest, then return the pan to a medium heat. Add the madeira and scrape the encrustation from the pan using a wooden spoon. Add the stock and bring to the boil. Reduce the sauce for 10 minutes until only around 3 fl oz remain. Add the dripping released while the meat was resting. With a whisk, beat the lumps of cold butter one by one into the sauce. Add a new lump of butter only when the previous one has been properly melted. The sauce should be thick and glossy. Season to taste with salt and pepper.

6 *serve*
In a frying pan, melt some butter over a medium heat. Meanwhile put the filet mignon on toast on warm plates. Fry the slices of foie gras for 30 seconds per side until the exterior is brown and crispy, the inside lukewarm and melting. Place the foie gras on the meat and spoon some sauce over that. Slice paper-thin slices of truffle over the plates.

1 *choose your meat*

Ask your butcher for 4 thin slices of porterhouse, a steak from the muzzle with a firm bite and generous fat marbling. Ask for the meat not to be cut straight, but at an angle with the grain, as you would cut salmon. Meat with a long thread is often tastier than when cut right on the thread.

2 *bake*

Allow the meat time to reach room temperature. Sprinkle the porterhouse with coarsely ground salt and pepper. Heat a frying pan over a high heat. Turn the heat down a little when the pan is hot. Melt a pat of butter, wait until the foam subsides and the butter starts to color. Grill the sirloins on a medium heat for 1-2 minutes on each side for rare (3 minutes for medium-rare, 4 minutes for medium). Reduce the heat when it looks like the butter could burn.

3 *rest*

Take the meat from the oven and let it rest on a baking rack for 5 to 15 minutes, loosely wrapped in a 'tunnel' of aluminum foil, with a plate for collecting liquids below. Meanwhile make the sauce.

4 *sauce*

Take 1 tablespoon dripping from the pan, drain the rest, then return the pan to a medium heat. Add the peppercorns and lemon juice. Scrape the encrustation from the pan using a wooden spoon. Allow the sauce to simmer for 2-3 minutes. With a whisk, beat the lumps of cold butter one by one into the sauce. Add a new lump of butter only when the previous one has properly melted. The sauce should be thick and glossy. Season to taste with salt and pepper.

5 *serve*

Serve the porterhouse slices on a warm plate and serve the sauce in a separate bowl. Delicious with crusty bread.

A nice fresh steak sauce **with lime and pickled green peppercorns. The acids give a nice counterbalance to the full-fat butter sauce.**

PREPARATION TIME: 15 MINUTES

INGREDIENTS
SERVES 4

21 ounces porterhouse, in 4 slices
butter

SAUCE
1 tablespoon green peppercorns (pot, pickled in vinegar)
juice of 3 limes
1 ¾ ounces ice-cold, unsalted butter, cut into lumps

ALSO:
aluminum foil

Many dishes are named after the 12th district of Paris, the Bercy district, which used to be the epicenter of the wine trade. Of course the wine also flowed freely at the restaurants in the neighborhood, at the table, and in the kitchen. This Beurre Bercy (sauce with fish stock) is based on shallots cooked with white (!) wine. The original version from many years ago also contained poached marrow, cut into cubes.

PREPARATION TIME: 20 MINUTES

INGREDIENTS
SERVES 4

4 rump steaks
butter

SAUCE
17 fl oz white wine
3 small shallots, finely chopped
2 tablespoons beef stock (canned)
2 tablespoons ice cold unsalted butter
3 tablespoons finely chopped
flat-leaf parsley
juice of ½ lemon

ALSO:
aluminum foil

1 choose your meat
Ask your butcher for rump steak (or sirloin steak), preferably cut from the middle, 1 inch thick and 5-7 ounces each. This sauce is also excellent with grilled rib-eye steak or a thick sirloin.

2 sauce
In a steel pan, mix the wine and shallot shreds and cook over a high heat for 10 minutes until reduced to half. Add the broth. With a whisk, beat 1 tablespoon of butter into the sauce. Add the next bit of butter only after the previous one has already melted. The sauce should be thick and glossy. Stir in the parsley and lemon juice. Season to taste with salt and pepper. Keep the sauce warm.

3 bake
Allow the meat time to reach room temperature. Sprinkle the steaks with coarsely ground salt and pepper. Heat a frying pan over a high heat. Turn the heat down a little when the pan is hot. Melt a pat of butter, wait until the foam subsides and the butter starts to color. Fry the steak on a medium heat for 1-2 minutes on each side for rare (3 minutes for medium-rare, 4 minutes for medium). Reduce the heat when it looks like the butter could burn.

4 rest
Let the steak rest for 5 minutes, loosely wrapped in aluminum foil.

5 serve
Serve the steaks on warm plates, topped with lots of gravy. Serve with crusty bread.

1 *choose your meat*

Ask your butcher for 4 thick slices of fillet steak. Preferably cut from the middle, 1 inch thick and 5-7 ounces each. Alternative: (cheaper) rump steak.

2 *bake*

Allow the steak time to reach room temperature. Brush the steak with olive oil and sprinkle with salt and pepper. Heat a frying pan over a high heat. Turn the heat down a little when the pan is hot. Melt a pat of butter, wait until the foam subsides and the butter starts to color. Fry the steak for 2 minutes on each side for rare (3 minutes for medium-rare, 4 minutes for medium). Reduce the heat when it looks like the butter could burn. Turn the meat with tongs and fry again for the same amount of time. Just before the steaks are ready, continue with step 3.

3 *flambé*

Add some extra butter to the pan. Switch the extractor off (otherwise the flames could reach into the extractor) and hold a lid in your hand to extinguish the fire in the pan if it should get too fierce. As soon as the butter has melted, pour a shot of cognac over the steaks. Ignite the alcohol vapors and fry for another 30 seconds after the flames have been extinguished. Alternative method: heat the cognac in a soup ladle by holding it above a small flame. Ignite the alcohol vapors (or hold the spoon slightly skew over the flame). Pour the flaming brandy over the steaks.

4 *rest*

Let the steak rest for 5 minutes, loosely wrapped in aluminum foil.

5 *serve*

Serve the steaks on warm plates. Serve with fries or white bread and lettuce.

A steak for meat lovers that prefer flame grilling. A dash of brandy in the pan and a splash on the meat. Good for an extra flame grilled taste and a spectacle in the kitchen.

PREPARATION TIME: 15 MINUTES

INGREDIENTS
SERVES 4

4 fillet steaks
1 clove garlic, crushed
butter
4 tablespoons cognac (or brandy)

ALSO:
aluminum foil

The meat from the small Japanese Wagyu cow is known for its superior taste, but unfortunately it is also very expensive. It is therefore recommended that you try one of the more affordable parts first. The porterhouse is very affordable and it is also an excellent steak.

PREPARATION TIME: 10 MINUTES

INGREDIENTS
SERVES 4

1 piece Wagyu porterhouse
of 10-14 ounces

ALSO:
aluminum foil

1 *choose your meat*

Ask your butcher for a nice piece of Wagyu steak, such as porterhouse (or order it online). Preferably buy one large piece. Wagyu is a very delicate piece of meat and the excessive fat marbling in the meat makes you feel full faster than with a regular piece of steak. A piece of 2 ½ – 3 ½ ounces should be sufficient for one person.

2 *bake*

Allow the meat time to reach room temperature. Sprinkle the porterhouse with coarsely ground salt and pepper. Heat a frying pan over a high heat. Turn the heat down a little when the pan is hot. Put the meat with tongs in the pan. Butter or olive oil is not required, as the meat contains enough fat on its own. Fry the porterhouse steak on a medium heat for 1-2 minutes on each side for rare (3 minutes for medium-rare, 4 minutes for medium). Keep an eye on the meat, because Wagyu fat melts quickly. Reduce the heat as soon as it looks like the fat could burn.

3 *rest*

Take the meat from the oven and let it rest on a baking rack for 5 to 15 minutes, loosely wrapped in a 'tunnel' of aluminum foil, with a plate for collecting liquids below.

4 *serve*

Place the porterhouse on a cutting board with a gutter. Cut the meat into four thin slices. Serve on warm plates.

STEAK

FROM FIELD TO TABLE

Side dishes and wine

Gratin Dauphinois

PREPARATION TIME: 15 MINUTES + 1 HOUR COOKING TIME

INGREDIENTS SERVES 4

2 ¾ POUNDS POTATOES, FIRM
20 FL OZ WHIPPING CREAM
1 TEASPOON (FRESHLY GRATED) NUTMEG
ALSO: OVEN DISH

PREPARATION: Preheat the oven to 350°F. Peel the potatoes and rinse them under cold running water. Cut the potatoes into thin slices of 1/10 inch thick each. Place the potato slices in layers in the baking dish. Pour in the cream, make sure all of the slices are properly covered. Sprinkle with nutmeg.
Place the oven dish on a grill in the middle of the oven. Bake the gratin for about 1 hour until tender and golden brown.

Lettuce with basic vinaigrette

PREPARATION TIME: 15 MINUTES

INGREDIENTS SERVES 4

2 HEADS OF LETTUCE
1 TABLESPOON HIGH QUALITY RED WINE VINEGAR
1 TEASPOON DIJON MUSTARD
2 TABLESPOONS OLIVE OIL (EXTRA VIRGIN)
2 TABLESPOONS SUNFLOWER OIL
ALSO NEEDED: SPINNER

PREPARATION: Fill a (clean!) sink or basin with cold water. Separate the lettuce leaves and wash them thoroughly, but be gentle because lettuce leaves are delicate and they bruise easily. Spin the lettuce dry in a salad spinner: crispy dry lettuce is half the success, otherwise the dressing will not stick well. An alternative, but slightly more primitive method: wrap the lettuce loosely in a kitchen towel or use an old-fashioned iron lettuce net. Go outside and shake the lettuce so that the liquid comes out. Put the lettuce in a bowl, cover the bowl and place it in the refrigerator. This will make the leaves extra cool and fresh and crispy. To make the vinaigrette, mix the vinegar and the salt together (salt dissolves very poorly in oil). Stir in the mustard. Continue beating with a fine whisk and add the sunflower oil and olive oil in a thin stream. The ratio of vinegar to oil is 1 to 3 or 1 to 4, depending on your preference. The vinaigrette should be lumpy. Season to taste with salt and pepper.
Just before serving, pour the vinaigrette over the salad and toss lightly with clean hands or with salad servers, making sure that each leaf is covered with a shiny layer of dressing. After the dressing has been added the lettuce leaves will quickly wilt. There are also countless variations: replace with white wine vinegar or with balsamic, for instance. Add lemon juice to bring out the taste of the olive oil.

Wild spinach with olive oil

PREPARATION TIME: 10 MINUTES

INGREDIENTS SERVES 4

1 ²/₃ POUNDS SPINACH
EXTRA VIRGIN OLIVE OIL

PREPARATION: Wash the delicate spinach leaves under cold running water or in a (clean!) sink or basin with cold water. Make sure that no sand is left behind. You do not need to remove the coarse stalks. In a pan, bring a small amount of water to the boil. Add the spinach and simmer for 30 seconds. The spinach must shrink, but must not become too tender. Remove the spinach with a skimmer and put it on a plate. Season to taste with pepper and coarsely ground sea salt and baste the spinach with some olive oil. Good quality spinach does not need anything else.

Braised celery

PREPARATION TIME: 20 MINUTES +
30-45 MINUTES WAITING TIME

INGREDIENTS SERVES 4

1 BUSH CELERY
2 SHALLOTS
1 CLOVE GARLIC
10 FL OZ BEEF BROTH
BUTTER

Roasted carrots from the oven

PREPARATION TIME: 10 MINUTES +
45 MINUTES COOKING TIME

INGREDIENTS SERVES 4

1 BUNDLE CARROTS
2 TABLESPOONS OLIVE OIL
4 CLOVES GARLIC
4 SPRIGS ROSEMARY
ALSO: GRIDDLE

PREPARATION: Preheat the oven to 350°F. Cut off the foliage, but leave a small piece of green at the top of the carrot. Scrape the carrots under cold running water and peel them using a vegetable peeler. Spread the carrots out on a baking sheet. Drizzle with olive oil and season with freshly ground salt and pepper. Place rosemary and whole garlic cloves between the carrots and place the baking tray in the middle of the oven. Grill the carrots for about 45 minutes.

PREPARATION: Separate the celery stalks and cut the tops off. Remove any stiff threads with a vegetable peeler. Cut the stalks into pieces of 1 ½ – 2 inches. Rub the inside with salt and pepper. Peel and chop the shallots. Melt the butter in a heavy saucepan. Sauté the shallots over a medium heat for 3-5 minutes until tender and light in color. Stir in the celery pieces and let them simmer for 5 to 10 minutes until the celery is also light in color.
Pour in enough stock to only just cover the celery. Place a lid on the pan and let it simmer for another 30-45 minutes over a low heat, until the stems are very tender. Add extra broth (or hot water) as needed to make sure that it does not boil dry.

Perfect hand-cut fries

PREPARATION: 10 MINUTES +
PREPARATION TIME: 50 MINUTES

INGREDIENTS SERVES 4

1 ²/₃ POUNDS POTATOES
50 FL OZ SUNFLOWER OIL
(OR OTHER VEGETABLE OIL)

ALSO:
DEEP FRYER WITH A BASKET
OR SLOTTED SPOON, PAPER TOWELS

PREPARATION: **peeling** Thinly peel the potatoes or use them peel and all, but then make sure to scrub the potatoes properly under cold, running water. Using a sharp knife, cut the potatoes into slices and then into strips. The thickness depends on your preference: do you prefer larger fries as is the custom in Belgium, or do you prefer French fries? Irrespective of your preference, make sure that all of the fries are roughly the same so that they can cook evenly. Rinse the potato strips for 2-3 minutes under cold, running water to remove the starch, so that the fries can cook better. Keep the potatoes submerged in water until you use them, to prevent them from discoloring. Blot the fries dry in a dish cloth or paper kitchen towels.

pre-frying (not necessary for very thin fries). Heat the oil in a deep fryer to 320°F (check the temperature with a probe). The oil will bubble slightly. Fry the fries for 5 minutes until they start floating on the surface – make sure that they do not discolor. Fry in small batches to prevent the oil from cooling down too much. Allow the oil to heat up before adding the next batch. Use a slotted spoon to remove the fries from the deep fryer, or turn them over directly from the basket onto a thick layer of paper towels. Drain and cool.
frying Heat the oil to 355°F (constant bubbling). Fry the fries in small portions for 2 to 3 minutes until crispy and golden brown. Allow the fries to drain in a colander with a double layer of paper towels. Sprinkle with coarse sea salt. Delicious with (homemade) mayonnaise.

TIP Try to use large potatoes that are specifically intended for making fries, which are available at some of the better-stocked greengrocers. Some types of boiling potatoes are not very suitable as they contain high levels of sugar, which can cause fries to actually taste bitter.

Fries à la Heston Blumenthal

British head chef Heston Blumenthal (The Fat Duck restaurant), well known for his molecular cuisine, has done an exhaustive study on how to make the perfect French fries. He concluded that the following types of potatoes should be used: Arran Victoryn or Maris Piper, cut into ½ inch thick strips. The secret of the Blumenthal method is to let the fries dry out during two ice-cold stages to remove excessive moisture and to make the fries extra crispy.

He cooks the potato strips in salted water, gently at first, until they nearly crack. He then carefully removes the fries from the water, allows them to cool down and then puts them in the refrigerator to cool down further. The fries are then fried in peanut oil at 265°F, until lightly colored. Drain, cool and refrigerate. The fries are then fried again at 375°F until golden brown. This method may take longer, but the results are surprising: crispy-crunchy on the outside and creamy-soft on the inside.

Homemade mayonnaise

**PREPARATION TIME:
10 MINUTES**

INGREDIENTS SERVES 4

1 EGG YOLK
1 TABLESPOON LEMON JUICE
1 TABLESPOON MUSTARD
7 FL OZ VEGETABLE OIL WITH A NEUTRAL FLAVOR
(E.G. SUNFLOWER OIL)
ALSO: WHISK OR BLENDER

PREPARATION: Important: all of the ingredients and the kitchen equipment must be at room temperature! In a bowl, whisk together the egg yolk, lemon juice, mustard and some finely ground salt and pepper. Continue to whisk and slowly add the oil in a thin stream until the sauce has thickened. The mayonnaise must be lumpy and stick to the convex side of a spoon.

TIP a blender also works well. Mix the yolk with seasoning for 1 minute in the blender. Pour some oil in a thin stream while the blender is running. Wait until the oil has been included before adding more until the correct consistency has been reached.

Roasted cherry tomatoes

**PREPARATION TIME: 10 MINUTES
+ 15 MINUTES COOKING TIME**

INGREDIENTS SERVES 4

4 VINES OF CHERRY TOMATOES
OLIVE OIL
2 CLOVES GARLIC
2 SPRIGS OF MINT
4 SPRIGS PARSLEY
ALSO: OVEN DISH

PREPARATION: Preheat the oven to 390°F. While still on the vine, place the tomatoes in an oven-proof dish. Drizzle with olive oil and chopped (or crushed) garlic. Sprinkle with freshly ground salt and pepper.
Roast the tomatoes in the oven for 10-15 minutes, until they burst and the juice is released. Pick the parsley and mint from the sprigs and chop them fine, then sprinkle over the tomatoes when taken from the oven. Serve with bread to dip into the sauce.

Rosemary roast potatoes

PREPARATION: 10 MINUTES + 45 MINUTES COOKING TIME

INGREDIENTS SERVES 4

30 OUNCES WAXY POTATOES
OLIVE OIL
4 CLOVES GARLIC, HALVED
1 TABLESPOON FINELY CHOPPED ROSEMARY

PREPARATION: Preheat the oven to 430°F. Scrub the potatoes clean under cold, running water. Pat the potatoes dry with paper towels. Cut them into quarters (in equal parts). Peel and halve the garlic. Place the potatoes on a baking sheet or in a baking dish with the oil, garlic and rosemary. Place the potatoes in the middle of the oven and roast for 45 minutes or a little longer until cooked and golden brown. Turn them over halfway through the cooking time. Before serving, sprinkle with some crispy fleur de sel or coarsely ground sea salt. Delicious with (homemade) mayonnaise.

Pommes Parisiennes

PREPARATION TIME: 45 MINUTES

INGREDIENTS SERVES 4

2 ¼ POUNDS WAXY POTATOES
½ BUNCH PARSLEY
BUTTER (OPTIONAL)
ALSO: MELON BALLER
(ALSO KNOWN AS THE PARISIENNE SCOOP)

PREPARATION: Peel the potatoes and rinse them under cold, running water. Using the melon baller, scoop balls from the raw potatoes (practice may be needed at first). Place the balls immediately in a bowl with cold water to prevent the potatoes from discoloring. The potato leftovers can be used to make mashed potatoes or to bind a vegetable soup.
Boil the potato balls in plenty of water with some salt for 10 minutes until al dente. Meanwhile, pluck the parsley leaves and roughly chop them. Drain the potatoes, add a knob of butter (optional) and add the parsley. Carefully shake the pan to mix the parsley. Variation: After cooking, allow the potatoes to cool slightly and to dry somewhat. Stir-fry in butter until golden brown.

What is the perfect wine for the perfect steak? According to the well-known Dutch wine writer Harold Hamersma, author of *De Grote Hamersma*, the annual wine merchants' guide in the Netherlands, there are actually many options available and sometimes (surprisingly!) a good white wine fits the bill perfectly.

"What goes best with a good piece of red meat? The simplest answer is: Cabernet Sauvignon wines and Cabernet Sauvignon dominated wines, which go well with almost anything. Red meat is slightly sweet, and you can taste the sweetness of the cassis and blackberries in Cabernet Sauvignon, even with 20% alcohol. The two tastes complement each other very well. The oak used to mature these wines is often aged to provide an extra spicy flavor. You can opt for a Cabernet Sauvignon from France, but the ones from the new world such as Chile and Australia are also good, if slightly sweeter because of the use of more blackcurrants.

There are also many other options available. When you enjoy a fine piece of steak in Spain you will most likely want to enjoy a Spanish classic such as Tempranillo wines that are produced in the best Spanish wine regions such as Priorat and Ribera del Duero. These are also valiant, firm, and full-bodied wines that go well with a good steak. Make sure not to take a fruity young wine, but rather an oak-matured wine, i.e. wines that were made to be good. Just like your steak you are looking for good earthy tones. The crispy fried fat layer of a sirloin steak goes very well with the earthy tones of a wine matured in wood. Mushrooms, truffles ... This is the kind of sensation you are looking for. A nice big piece of red meat is a wonderful excuse for dusting off your best bottle of red wine in the cellar. In Italy they will not hesitate one moment about what to enjoy with a good piece of steak: Chianti Classico Reserva, which is a perfect combination. Tip: Barolo also goes well with a marbled rib-eye from the grill. The touch of acidity of a Barolo combines well with the fat of the steak. Malbec, an Argentinian red wine, goes very well with grilled Argentine steaks, e.g. a T-bone steak with

Some tips from Hamersma: sense and nonsense about wine

Decanting?

"Yes, that can be very useful, but only in young wines as they are still locked in. Young wines often benefit from a shock of oxygen. If you do not have a carafe, simply pour the wine into a pot or a measuring jug, then pour it back into the bottle through a funnel. Decanting is not necessary for older wines. A wine that is 20 or 30 years old must be kept in an environment that is low in oxygen and a shock of oxygen is not good for it. Airing without the cork is also nonsense. It does not have any effect because the opening is too small."

Room temperature?

"Wine is often served too warm. The term 'room temperature' comes from a time when the temperature in the living room used to be 60 to 65 degrees Fahrenheit. These days we all have central heating and room temperature has gone up to 70 degrees Fahrenheit or more. Keeping wines next to an open fireplace also has a very negative effect on the wine. After all, you would not keep a bottle of strawberries next to the fireplace, that would completely destroy them. There is currently a trend for drinking cooler red wine, sometimes even as cool as 50 to 55°F."

chimichurri sauce, which is also slightly sweet and peppery. A good guide is to always drink a wine from the same region as the dish that you are eating.

The thicker your meat, the 'thicker' your wine should be. A large prime rib from the oven needs a powerful wine, while steak frites, often made of thin steaks, goes well with a young Côte du Rhone, based on Shiraz Grenache. In my opinion a red Beaujolais goes well with steak tartare. Make sure that you choose a good winemaker, e.g. one of the ten Beaujolais Crus, such as Fleurie or Brouilly. Or even better: enjoy a Morgon, one of the most full-bodied Beaujolais Crus wines. Beaujolais goes well with a casual dish such as steak tartare. Steak sandwich? Opt for a lightly chilled red Valpolicella or Beaujolais.

Red Burgundy also goes well with steak and many other dishes, but it's not my first choice. The wine is often too elegant, too subtle, which fits better with chicken or guinea fowl. I prefer a Pinot Noir from the New World, as they have more of a bite. Some of my favorite wine books, such as the 'magic' book *What you drink with what you eat* by Andrew Dornenburg and Karen Page, also recommend these wines as logical choices.

A classic steak could also go with a Bordeaux, or even a Margaux or Latour, but some experts consider them as a bit too tangy. When you uncork a top quality wine, make sure to enjoy it with a steak that was prepared with the minimum of bells and whistles.

Another important factor is what you eat with your meat, e.g. which vegetables, what kind of sauce? And what goes best with a Béarnaise filet mignon? Egg sauce, high levels of butter, acetic acid, chervil and tarragon? This is often the subject of debate as it is difficult to find the right combination. Béarnaise is prepared with so many herbs and acids, which you want to wash down with a wine, and you may not always feel like uncorking a matured red wine.

I made a great discovery recently: White wine, not red, goes very well with Béarnaise filet mignon. To be precise, a Domaine de Bellivière 'Les Rosiers', 2006 Jasnières from Eric Nicolas ($25,00). It seems that the ripe, fruity, soft-spicy,

How to read a wine list in a restaurant

"If you trust the restaurant, ask the sommelier if they can recommend something. For example: 'Do you have something red that is very reasonably priced?' You could also ask the sommelier for a specific type that you enjoy. Cabernet Sauvignon has a fruity taste because of the blackberries, while Merlot is is somewhat plummy and Shiraz is often peppery. Sauvignon Blanc is often more pointed, fresher, and bolder, while Chardonnay has a very broad spectrum, yet tends to be light tropical or yellow fruity. Naturally it also depends on the vine that the grapes came from and whether the grapes were allowed to ripen on the wood. You can describe to the sommelier what taste you prefer and ask them to recommend something."

Wine package?

"We live in a country that is still learning. We have only been drinking wine with our dinner for the past twenty or thirty years. That's not very long if you think about it. You can see, however, that we are very eager to learn. The proportion of good wines has gone up considerably in the Netherlands during the last few decades. Combining wine and food can sometimes lead to some excellent discoveries, but at the end of the day you should drink the wine that you feel like at the moment. At the end of the day it is up to you what you drink with fish, oysters, tenderloin or whatever."

Are there some combinations that should simply be avoided?

"Artichokes and spinach are always difficult to combine with wine as they contain lots of iron, which does not go well with wine. Peanuts and peanut sauces are also always a no-no."

and especially the tight, super fine acidity of the Chenin Blanc grape complements filet mignon and Béarnaise very well, and even enhances the taste. A bloody red Béarnaise filet mignon with a pale white Loire. But it is always said that "red wine goes with red meat"? I tried this twice more... and both times the wine worked very well. A top quality Chardonnay from the New World also goes very well with Béarnaise. You must also think very carefully what to drink with a dominant sauce such as a traditional piccalilli, which I think also goes very well with a white wine. If you still want a red wine though, make sure to go young – less than five years old.

A steak with a cream sauce or a classic red wine sauce such as bordelaise demands a big red. You also can't go wrong if you drink the wine that you used to prepare the sauce. This does not need to be expensive wine, a nice bottle of Cabernet Sauvignon for five or six dollars is often good enough.

The best steak experience I ever had was at the legendary Gibson's in Chicago. This is a typical steakhouse with wood paneling and pictures of celebrities on the wall. The whole place looks classy and it is always full.

'Party Hamersma, table is ready!' is their typical call to alert customers that their table is ready. The meat, superior Black Angus steaks from sustainable farms in the neighborhood, is matured for forty days. The lady steak alone weighs three ounces.

I ate a sirloin steak of nine ounces. It was prepared in a very basic manner, and I literally devoured it. I couldn't help but think: this may become a long night yet, but I will sleep like a baby. We drank a Zinfandel, the national pride of America, by Ridge from California. After all, when you spend so much money on one steak you are compelled to also drink a top quality wine. This was an unforgettable combination."

House wine?

"A good restaurant sees its house wine as its best advertisement. You will notice that the quality of house wines are on the up. With wine by the glass, for instance, some very good solutions have been found for vacuum-packing the wine. I am a strong supporter of this. I am in favor of anything that makes wine more accessible to the masses."

Young or old wine?

"The simple rule is: if a young wine does not taste good it will also not taste good when it is old. If a young wine has potential to be stored it must in principle already be a good drinking wine when it is young. Another misconception is that people often expect to drink nectar from the gods when they open an old bottle of wine. It is a fact that many people do not like the so-called secondary flavors. Some peole prefer fruity flavors over a slight animal-like smell or leather, tobacco, mushrooms. You need to understand how to appreciate this and it is really only meant for wine connoisseurs. Having said that, some wine connoisseurs prefer drinking young wines instead of older wines. This is a subject that could be very interesting to study."

Dutch wine?

"Each province currently has its own professional wine makers, but they all have very small parcels of land and as a result they are not commercially viable. The one aspect that they are very good at is developing wine tourism around the industry. The quality is constantly improving, but the prices are also quite high as the wines easily sell for between Euro 10 to Euro 15."

STEAK

FROM FIELD TO TABLE

Me and my steak

My favorite way to prepare...

'I'm completely against frying anything in margarine'

Culinary journalist Felix Wilbrink, winner of awards such as the Wina Born award (Wina Born is widely considered as the mother of Dutch gastronomy), has been frying his favorite steak in the same Xenos cast iron frying pan for more than 35 years.

NAME: FELIX WILBRINK,
CULINARY JOURNALIST FOR *DE TELEGRAAF*
(NATIONAL NEWSPAPER IN THE NETHERLANDS)
FAVORITE: RUMP STEAK (THICK RUMP)
HOW: *MEDIUM-RARE*

"One of my favorite neighborhood butchers is the De Wit butchery in Watergraafsmeer in the Netherlands. Herman de Wit, a true professional, still processes the entire animal with his own hands. He makes all of the sausages, pâtés, ham and the award-winning beef sausages all by himself. His beef comes from Meuse-Rhine-Issel and Roodbont.

My favorite steak is cut from the thick knuckle, which I prefer to the flat knuckle. I love a nice, thick slice of just over an inch and about 7 ounces, so somewhat on the luxurious side. It must not be too thin, because then it cooks too fast. I grill the steak in my trusty cast iron frying pan that I've had since I was 19 years old, when I first moved out of the house. I bought it at Xenos and it's got 'Made in Taiwan' printed on the bottom. Cast iron conducts heat very well.

When I put butter in the frying pan a sort of a star shape appears over the entire surface, which is a sign that the heat is evenly distributed. I always put a generous amount of fresh butter in the pan, preferably unsalted.

I do not use margarine, because I'm completely against frying anything in margarine. It is important to heat the meat slowly otherwise the butter will burn. I salt the meat in advance, because it promotes crust formation. I do not use any pepper because I've noticed that when you cook with pepper the meat becomes bitter. Once the meat is in the pan, it is a matter of playing with fire. When it seems like the heat is too much, I add some more butter, which cools down the pan and the dripping. Once it is done I set the steak aside to rest and I make a simple gravy by adding a few spoons of hot water to the dripping. After the meat is done I use a lovely coarse salt from Guerlande and only then do I add coarsely ground pepper.

I also like a lovely roast. I remember the roast beef that we used to eat every Sunday at the foster home where I grew up. My stepfather used to sharpen his knife and he used to concentrate hard as he sliced every piece of meat $\frac{1}{10}$ inch thick. We got exactly one slice per person, no more because we had to eat more from it later in the week. It was always so delicious, beautifully cooked, red-pink and super tender.

My foster mother baked the meat the day before, on Saturday afternoon, in a large frying pan. On Sunday afternoon around noon, after church, she would put the pan on the smallest burner on an asbestos hot plate. I later learned that this was actually called slow cooking. She used to turn the meat frequently. After it was done she put the meat aside to rest while she made the gravy.

I used to love sitting on a yellow Brabantia stool with three legs and watch how she cooked. The kitchen was a nice, warm place for me. It is very possible that this laid the foundations for my current work as a food critic."

FELIX'S TIP: "WHEN IT SEEMS LIKE THE HEAT IS TOO MUCH, I ADD SOME MORE BUTTER, WHICH COOLS DOWN THE PAN AND THE DRIPPING."

Johan van Uden, butcher in Heemstede and one of the youngest ever winners of the prestigious Golden Butcher's Ring (a butcher's competition in the Netherlands), explains how he prepares his favorite sirloin steak.

NAME: JOHAN VAN UDEN,
BUTCHER CHATEAUBRIAND, HEEMSTEDE
FAVORITE: SIRLOIN STEAK
HOW: *SAIGNANT*

"Nearly twenty years ago I came through butcher training where I learned old school boning and slaughtering. After completing my butcher training in the Netherlands I continued with additional training and work placement in Belgium and Paris. I worked with French butchers and at the Paris delicatessen Fauchon. It's fantastic to see how serious the people over there are when it comes to eating and the quality of their food. I still drive one Sunday every month to Rungis night market in Paris for our restaurant/butchery to look for special products. Belgium is a great country for steak frites. And of course Paris with its innumerable bistros and brasseries. My favorite is the sirloin. Beautifully marbled, with a nice layer of fat on the outside. I love Aberdeen Angus, which we import directly from Scotland. There the animals have enough land available, so they are fed 100% natural grass. And you can taste it. In the Netherlands we often eat beef while it is too fresh. A good steak must be left on the bone to dry-age for at least three weeks. In the past meat was simply left in the barn to mature. Nowadays, we use a special cold rooms and we call it dry aging. The temperature and humidity in the dry-aged cell is closely monitored. During the maturation process the dry-aged beef loses a great deal of moisture, which makes it even more tender and gives it an unrivaled taste. In cities such as New York and Sydney dry aging is very popular and there you can even see complete carcasses as they ripen in refrigerated display cabinets in butcheries and steakhouses, which is amazing to see. We recently became one of the first butcheries in the Netherlands with a dry-age cell. Anybody can buy dry-aged meat directly from our store or through our online store at www.dryagedvlees.nl.

Patience is the key to baking the perfect steak. Often people take a cold steak and put it in a pan that is much too hot. When you cook the meat too quickly over excessive heat you're effectively killing the steak. A steak is a muscle and it literally shrinks together. The butter also burns when the pan is too hot, which causes a bitter taste. The best piece of sirloin steak is the fat on the outside, which is exactly why I always cook the steak first of all on the fatty side. When the fat melts it gives the meat extra flavor. When you use top-quality beef, steak is also delicious when it is raw, such as the classic carpaccio. I'm very proud to say that I have been called the spiritual father of tapenade from Scotch Beef, with which I won the Golden Butcher's Ring. The creator of roulades and cordon bleu is also part of this illustrious butcher's fellowship. My tapenade is made with quality olive oil, Parmigiano Reggiano, chopped pine nuts, capers and freshly ground sea salt and pepper. The most important aspect is super tender meat, for which I use sirloin. The meat is also not ground by a machine, but always chopped by hand."

JOHAN'S TIP: "BE PATIENT. WHEN YOU COOK THE MEAT TOO QUICKLY OVER EXCESSIVE HEAT YOU'RE EFFECTIVELY KILLING THE STEAK."

'I love to eat meat while it is almost alive on my plate'

The American food blogger David Ciancio founded Steak Club 7 with six friends, a blog exclusively devoted to reviewing steakhouses in New York City.

NAME: DAVID CIANCIO,
CO-FOUNDER OF STEAK CLUB 7
FAVORITE: NEW YORK STRIP
HOW: *RARE*

"It started as a joke. We knew each other from the record industry: Rich 'Meat God', JoeC, Matty Winks, Jon, The Big PA and myself, nicknamed The Rev. The idea was that us seven guys had to go out to eat steaks together. No women allowed, no talking about work, just steaks. A club rule: Guests are not allowed (unless they are willing to pay the entire bill). After a few months we started the website Steak Club 7 (steakclub7.wordpress.com) with our findings. We received lots of comments from restaurants that invited us to come and eat there! Soon we became the number one steak website on the Internet. Since 2004 we've been going nearly every month, at least ten times a year, to a steak restaurant. Our mission is to visit all of the steakhouses in New York City. There is no other place in the world where you can eat steaks as good as this. We each take turns to be captain of the evening and select a restaurant. I always order the same thing: whiskey as an aperitif, Balvenie Scotch. The appetizer is bacon. A thick slice, crispy fried with barbecue sauce. Then I order a New York strip (sirloin steak), unless someone else wants to share a porterhouse of 2.6 pounds with me. We also critically examine the side dishes. Broccoli or spinach? Baked potatoes or fries? And what sauces are available on the table? My dessert is always the same: Chocolate Sundae (vanilla ice cream with hot chocolate sauce) and an espresso with black Sambuca. I'm the steak club sommelier. I really like a Cabernet and Shiraz from Italy, Argentina or Australia. My perfect steak? I like my steak to be properly seared on the outside and red and juicy on the inside. Screaming for life, almost as if it's still alive on my plate. I like that, it makes me remember that I am alive.

One of my best steak experiences was while I was living with my mother, when I was thirteen years old. We were sitting as a family in a steak restaurant in Detroit. My mom had had a few martinis and she was a little tipsy. The waiter asked how she wanted her steak. She replied: "I would prefer you to remove the horns, wipe his ass and put him on a plate... Rare will also be just fine.'

Peter Luger's Steakhouse is legendary in New York and, along with The Old Homestead, it is one of the oldest steakhouses in town. You get to enjoy great steaks in a classic setting. But my personal favorite is Marc Joseph Steakhouse on 261 Water Street, downtown Manhattan. The owner is one of the first ex-workers of Peter Luger who started his own business. Here you can enjoy the perfect porterhouse steak with a fantastic homemade steak sauce. The only time I ever ate a better T-bone steak was when I was in Florence in Italy. After you order the meat you can hear the chef chopping the steak. You cannot get any better than that."

DAVID'S TIP: "MY FAVORITE STEAK HOUSE IS MARC JOSEPH STEAKHOUSE IN NEW YORK. JOSEPH WAS ONE OF THE FIRST EX-WORKERS OF PETER LUGER WHO STARTED HIS OWN BUSINESS."

Arno Veenhof, butcher at the famous Amsterdam butchery and delicatessen Yolanda and Fred de Leeuw, is one of the few butchers in the Netherlands that sells the famous Wagyu beef.

NAME: ARNO VEENHOF,
BUTCHER AT YOLANDA AND FRED DE LEEUW, AMSTERDAM
FAVORITE: WAGYU PORTERHOUSE
HOW: *SAIGNANT*

"I come from a real butcher's family. When I was eleven, I started cutting in my father's butchery and at this time butchers still went to the cattle market to buy their own livestock. At home we always ate meat. In 2000 I took over the butchery Yolanda and Fred de Leeuw, which is the most famous butchery in Amsterdam. My aim is to work without compromise. I'm always looking for the most special products. For example, we sell Iberian pig, chickens from Bresse, fresh truffles and Rubia, a lesser-known Spanish breed of cattle. We are also one of the few butcheries in the Netherlands that sells Wagyu, the ultimate beef of Japanese origin. My predecessor, Fred de Leeuw, had already shown considerable interest in Wagyu towards the end of the 90s, basically before anyone in the Netherlands had ever heard of Wagyu. The Wagyu beef that I sell comes from Morgan Davis Ranch, a leading American Wagyu producer. Because of the history of Wagyu at our butchery I always have the first choice at my wholesaler, so I get the cattle with the most beautiful marbled fat. Intramuscular fat in the muscle mass is one of the most important qualities that I watch out for. Wagyu is expensive because the animals enjoy a richer, healthier diet, without antibiotics or hormones. This means that it takes longer for the meat to become well marbled, when the animal is ready for slaughter.

Because of the price, I use all of the parts and I make all kinds of meat products. We make salted meat and pastrami from the breast, for example. An item that is always very popular here is our Thai Wagyu meatballs. I consider it a sport to bring the less common parts to the attention of people. Our display cabinets also contain Wagyu porterhouse, which is normally only used as a pot roast. When baked the fat melts, which causes the meat to become soft and full flavored. I consider Wagyu porterhouse to be the ultimate steak.

I have noticed a trend that meat is increasingly being used as a sort of a garnish at meal time. I think that is a good development. I don't think the way that the organic industry deals with meat is sustainable. I believe in small scale, purity of race, and traceability. If you eat Wagyu, you do not need to eat as much meat as the high fat content means that you become full faster. Three to three and a half ounces is normally enough for one person. The small portions means that Wagyu is actually also affordable.

You always need to take your time when cooking Wagyu in brown, bubbly butter over a medium heat. Allow the meat to reach room temperature and rub it with coarse sea salt and crushed black pepper about an hour before you cook it. I prefer searing the meat, after which I put it in the oven at 260°F for a few minutes to reach a core temperature of 115°F. I prefer it beautifully red. Ideally I bake a bigger piece and serve it in slices for several people, instead of one steak each."

ARNO'S TIP: "BUY A LARGER PIECE OF STEAK AND SERVE IT IN SLICES SO THAT EVERYONE IN THE TABLE CAN EAT FROM IT, INSTEAD OF SERVING EACH A PIECE OF STEAK."

Boudewijn Roemers, a trainer at the SVO (Dutch Association for the Advancement of Butcher Training), loves steak from lesser known Roan cattle, preferably from the female because it contains more fat.

NAME: BOUDEWIJN ROEMERS, TRAINER AT THE SVO (DUTCH ASSOCIATION FOR THE ADVANCEMENT OF BUTCHER TRAINING)
FAVORITE: SIRLOIN STEAK
HOW: *MEDIUM-RARE*

"We hardly ever teach our students how to bone a carcass. As recently as 15 years ago, this was a mandatory part of the training, But as with anyone who is involved with professional training, we need to meet the demands of the market. Unfortunately in practice there isn't a need for butchers with this type of skill any more, which is a pity because a great skill of the trade is being lost. There are only a few butchers in the Netherlands who can bone a carcass completely. The real boning work is already finished in the slaughterhouses and at wholesalers these days. Butcheries receive the meat from that wholesalers, completely boned.

Our students only learn how to dissect the meat into cuts. They learn for example which are the most important parts of the topside to cut steaks from.

I have noticed that in restaurants waiters are struggling to say what kind of steak they have on their menu. Is it a knuckle? A Dutch steak? A fillet? This is why I prefer cooking my own steak at home. I love a steak that is slightly chewy. A steak cut from the sirloin has a bit of a bite. I love Roan cattle, which are powerful traditional Dutch animals with distinctive red-brown spots and a noble head. This breed is an improved version of the Meuse-Rhine-Issel cattle, which is a dual purpose race intended for dairy and meat production. These varieties have the most flavor and a nice solid muscle mass. I prefer cows over bulls because bulls and steers generally have a lower percentage of fat. I consider an animal with a slaughter weight of around 1200 pounds to be ideal. Heavier animals tend to be bodybuilders with no flavor.

I cook my perfect steak in liquid cooking butter, which can stand higher temperatures than ordinary butter. For extra flavor I also add melted lard or beef fat in a 50-50 ratio. Before I put the steak in the pan, I rub the meat with a mixture of coarse sea salt, coarsely ground four seasons pepper and herbs, including mace. The steak should be two fingers thick and weigh approximately 7 ounces and I cook it for five minutes because I prefer medium-rare. First of all I cook both sides for a minute and a half each over a medium-high temperature. Then I cook each side another minute each over a low temperature.

I always serve the steaks on warmed plates, which I warm up by placing them under hot running water, or in the oven at 250°F. While the meat is resting I place a piece of cheese on the meat to melt. The cheese must not have too strong a flavor, because the cheese must not be dominant. A suitable cheese for example is Port Salut, a young, mild and creamy cheese from France."

BOUDEWIJN'S TIP: "FOR EXTRA FLAVOR I USE LIQUID BUTTER AND MELTED LARD OR BEEF FAT IN A 50-50 RATIO."

Head chef Leon Mazairac only really learned how to fry steaks when he started working with Alain Ducasse in Paris where the ultimate chateaubriand is served with a perfectly whipped Béarnaise.

NAME: LEON MAZAIRAC, HEAD CHEF AND OWNER OF PODIUM RESTAURANT IN UTRECHT, IN THE NETHERLANDS
FAVORITE: CHATEAUBRIAND WITH BÉARNAISE
HOW: *SAIGNANT* OR *BLEU*

"When I worked with Alain Ducasse in his three-star restaurant in Paris of the same name I learned a lot about the essence of meat. One of his specialties is pièce de boeuf Rossini. This is a rib for several people, served with an entire lobe of foie gras, truffle sauce and soufflé potatoes, and carved at the table. This dish must be ordered when you make your reservation. The pièce de boeuf is taken from the fridge a few hours in advance to bring it to room temperature before it is prepared on a grill on the cooker. This makes the fat nice and soft and it is already starting to drip a little bit onto the plate before you place it on the pan. Cooling is of course necessary for hygiene purposes, but deadly for the taste.

For me nothing beats a chateaubriand Béarnaise, not a double filet mignon as is often served in the Netherlands, but the top of the fillet. I usually order it saignant. Bleu is also good, but then you need to make sure that the meat is of absolute premium quality. Everywhere I have worked the meat is seasoned with pepper and salt both before and after baking, which helps develop the flavor. I use finely ground white pepper and some salt and butter and grapeseed oil as fat. I allow the oil to heat up first, after which I add a pat of butter, immediately followed by the meat to sear it. I cook over a high heat at first to allow the butter to draw into the meat. Do not sear the sides because that will only dry out the meat. It is essential for the pan to be hot. Many people do four steaks at the same time in a pan that is not hot enough. When you do this the temperature of the pan quickly drops from 300°F to 140°F, which is not good at all and you end up stewing the meat instead of baking it, which makes the meat gray. When you put the meat in the pan you must hear a hissing sound. Never shake the pan and do not baste it with dripping. You can do that with a roast, but with anything as lean as a filet mignon and it does not really have much taste. After searing I put the meat in the oven for a few minutes (hot area at 310°F). Crucially: after searing the meat, let it rest for about 10 minutes or so before you put it in the oven. Steaks served in average cafes are often baked à la minute, which should not be done as the meat needs time to rest. Another great misconception is that the steak must be completely hot on your plate. Lukewarm is fine, only your fries should be piping hot.

Béarnaise is often prepared in a bain marie in the Netherlands, but I find it too fluffy for my taste. You need to keep a close eye on the pan and the sauce, just like mayonnaise, which I prepare it in the traditional way. I mix it in the shape of an eight, over a low heat in a copper saucepan. The eggs with castric (boiled vinegar with tarragon) must first become thicker and solidify and only then should you add the butter. In my opinion the tastiest steak sauce is Béarnaise with chopped tomato."

LEON'S TIP: "IT IS A POPULAR MISCONCEPTION THAT THE STEAK MUST BE COMPLETELY HOT."

How does the famous restaurant critic Johannes van Dam prefer to eat his steak, and what knife does he use?

NAME: JOHANNES VAN DAM, CULINARY JOURNALIST
FAVORITE: SIRLOIN STEAK
HOW: *BLEU*

"During the past few years interest in the brasserie kitchen has been rekindled. More and more restaurants are beginning to serve simple and well prepared steaks. I think this is a very welcome development. The quality of the steaks is also very variable. You do not have to be a gourmet to recognize the quality of a good piece of steak. Even blindfolded you can taste the difference between a cheap piece of steak from an overweight animal and a more expensive piece of steak from a meat boutique. The perfect steak is slightly crispy on the outside and is juicy and tender on the inside. It also goes without saying that the steak must have a good meat flavor, which starts with the race and the cut. Wagyu muzzle is a great piece of steak, but the same cut from an old dairy cow is not edible. I prefer beautifully marbled sirloin with a fatty rind and with the right thickness. I think that Charolais is too big an animal and the meat does not really have much taste. Wagyu, Simmental and Aberdeen Angus are all full of flavour. I like to eat my steak bleu, which means seared on the outside with the inside raw, but warm. It is important for the meat to be of excellent quality and for it to be properly cut. Unfortunately there is much confusion about the terms that indicate the doneness of your meat. I have often found when asking the waiter to prepare my steak bleu that I'm faced with a look of incomprehension and then I get a medium-rare steak instead of bleu. My favorite sirloin is at least two fingers thick. I do not like those thin French minute steaks, which dry out very quickly. I prefer cooking with ghee, which is Indian clarified butter and can bought in a can at most oriental stores. Ghee is made by melting and heating the butter until all of the water has evaporated, without browning the butter. Because it does not contain any water, there is no splashing and it can be heated to a considerable degree without burning. It has the same properties as frying in oil, but you get the lovely nutty taste of butter through prolonged heating. I fry in a steel pan or cast iron pan and I never use stainless steel pans because food tends to stick to much on them. Also important: do not prick the steak, but turn it over with tongs. One of my pet peeves is the knife that you use: never cut a steak with a serrated steak knife, rather use a smooth, sharp knife. I am the proud owner of a collection of more than three hundred pocket knives and I even own an antiquarian six-volume encyclopedia of knives from 1904 (*La Coutellerie des origines à nos jours* by Camille Pagé) in the display cabinet. My favorite pocket knife is Laguiole Rossignol from the French producer Thérias & l'Econome, knife makers since 1819, established in Thiers, the center of knife production in France. The quality and the finish of these pocket knives are unmatched. Anyone who cuts a piece of steak with a serrated knife and with a smooth, sharp knife can clearly see the difference. When you cut with a serrated knife you always end up with meat juices on your plate and as a result the meat loses its juiciness and flavor.
I enjoy eating a good steak on bread with a little butter and without gravy because a good steak does not need any sauce."

JOHANNES' TIP: "MY FAVORITE FRYING MEDIUM IS GHEE, AN INDIAN CLARIFIED BUTTER WITH A NICE NUTTY FLAVOR."

A steak from the most exuberant vegan in the Netherlands. For anyone who wants to spend one day without eating any meat.

NAME: LISETTE KREISCHER, AUTHOR OF *VEGGIE IN PUMPS, GUIDE TO AN ECO-FABULOUS LIFESTYLE*
FAVORITE: SEITAN STEAK
HOW: WITH FRIES AND VEGANAISE ON THE SIDE

"I am a true herbivore and I enjoy eating vegetables. If you really want to treat me, give me some marinated asparagus. When I was ten, I stopped eating meat because I started thinking, how can I pet animals during the day and then eat their flesh in the evening? I come from an ordinary meat-potatoes-vegetables family. We ate steak with gravy, served at the table in a large frying pan with slices of white bread, full of gravy. I thought that the salt and fat of the sandwich with gravy was more delicious than the meat.

When I was twenty I decided to also stop eating dairy and I became a vegan as I have become more knowledgeable on how the meat, fish and egg industry worked and I thought it did not feel right. I have since discovered sufficient alternatives. I noticed that it was good for my body, my intestines and my skin and I had more energy.

A true vegan does not use any animal products, not even any clothing made from leather. Some hardcore vegans identify completely with the pain of animals. They even go so far as to avoid talking to any meat eaters. I do not go that far, even though I do not like the fact that animals are killed.

The production of two pounds of meat costs about the same as 15 to 20 pounds of grain. For soybeans it goes as high as 35 pounds for every two pounds of meat. Very inefficient. Soy often comes from the Amazon region where people die from malnutrition. They cannot even make use of their own land. Meat is harmful to the environment. Eighteen percent of total CO_2 emissions are accounted for by the meat and feed industry. This is more than the emissions from all types of transport put together. Last, but certainly not least, is the suffering of the animals with intensive livestock farming. Just look at all the shocking undercover footage available on the Internet.

I like to eat vegetable proteins, such as seitan, nuts and seaweed. Seaweed is for instance very rich in high-quality protein and it is environmentally friendly to grow.

There are also many kinds of seaweed, the sea is full of them. The average vegan considers salt and fat to be delicious and I make a lard variety for vegans from coconut oil, olive oil, cloves, salt, bay leaf and other herbs. The fatty flavor is obtained from the coconut oil, mixed with olive oil. When you add tofu, marinated in a salty soy sauce such as shoyu, and then bake it, it tastes fantastic. You can also make crackling from tofu or sun-dried tomato, crispy-fried in lard. You can also make bacon from tempeh, which is fermented soybeans.

My favorite veggie steak is not made from soy products such as tofu because I try to consume soy sparingly due to the impact it has on the environment. I prefer seitan steak, which is made from wheat gluten and has a firm, meat-like fiber structure and a savory flavor. First marinate in shoyu, then bake in lard and deglaze with red wine. This also goes very well with fries made from organic potatoes and with deliciously creamy 'Veganaise', which is made from apple, vinegar, mustard, olive oil and oat cream (a sort of sour cream, but without milk). Meat substitutes are good for people who are switching, but I do not eat it often myself. I would much rather eat seitan steak with homemade fries."

LISETTE'S TIP: "CRACKLING FROM TOFU OR SUN-DRIED TOMATO, BAKED IN VEGAN LARD UNTIL CRISPY."

STEAK

FROM FIELD TO TABLE

Famous Restaurants

Aberdeen Angus
Côte de Boeuf
5 weken dry aged
Lyndall farm

Ripened reputations

At the world-famous Peter Luger in New York you do not eat any old ordinary steak, but a porterhouse that is three fingers thick and weighs at least 2 pounds, served on a sizzling hot plate with dripping and gravy with butter. As a starter: a thick slice of crispy fried bacon. Eat your heart out.

Peter Luger Steakhouse – 'since 1887' – is an institution. Local connoisseurs say that "they defined the New York steak". The restaurant is located in the trendy part of Brooklyn, exactly one bridge away from downtown Manhattan. It is a minor miracle that the restaurant managed to become the most famous steakhouse in New York (it has been rated number one for the past 24 years running according to the Zagat restaurant guide), and not just because of its notoriously grumpy reception. The place is full, every day, seven days a week. If you want to eat at the steakhouse, you need to make a reservation at least six weeks in advance, but you will most likely have to wait an hour before you are seated. They do not accept credit cards, which is the standard method of payment for most Americans. Another cherished peculiarity: they have not employed a female waitress yet. Even taking into account that this is a New York steakhouse, the choice of steaks is very limited. At Peter Luger they basically have only one dish on the menu: the legendary Luger Porterhouse steak, which can be ordered for one, two, three or even four people. That steak is incredibly well made.

Classics

The waiters – who all wear starched aprons, impeccable white shirts with rolled-up sleeves, and a classic black bow tie – look like they have been working there since its inception. All of the experienced waiters work very fast to take your orders in a professional, yet friendly manner. Regular guests start their lunch or dinner with an appetizer consisting of a thick slice of crispy fried bacon – one of the other Luger classics – eaten with a sandwich and homemade sweet and sour BBQ sauce, served in a porcelain gravy boat. The Porterhouse – a generous 3 pounds for two people – is the norm at Luger, served in pre-cut slices, with the bone.

The meat literally sizzles on the tray, which is heated under a glowing grill, and guests can even bake their own steak a little bit longer if they find it to be too raw on the edge of the tray (which the waiter assured me is 390°F). An interesting detail: the plate with the steak (with a cup under the plate) is served on an inclined tray so that the golden fat (butter and dripping) runs down to baptize the steak. Diehards pour the dripping into a shot glass and drink this down to the very last drop to put their cardiology system to a severe test. Even without this folklore, Luger steak still has an indestructible reputation. The meat is super tender, with a crispy, deep brown crust and perfectly baked pinkish-red (or any other cuisson the guest prefers). The noisy, informal setting with German dark-wood paneling makes the Luger experience complete.

Selection

It is not necessarily the way the steaks prepared that make them so unique. As is the case in most steakhouses in New York, they use a broiler grill – an incredibly warm grill that heats the steak from above at a temperature as high as 2370°F so that the crust grills to a perfect crispy brown in one minute.

The crux lies in the selection of meat. Luger only uses Prime Beef of the highest quality, certified by the Ministry of Agriculture. The carcasses are delivered to the restaurant several times a week. Jody Storch, granddaughter of Sol Forman who had taken over the declining Luger restaurant in 1950 (established by the German immigrant Peter Luger), is responsible for the daily selection of meat, along with her mother and aunt. "My grandfather ensured that my grandmother became an expert in steaks during the first few years," said Jody. "She has been taking me to the meat market in downtown Manhattan since I was 10 years old. Our suppliers have know me since

I was a baby." The meat is dry-aged for the first three to four weeks while still on the bone on racks the same height as a person, in a deep cellar 33 feet below the steakhouse. Their own butchers cut the meat from the bone. Luger only serves Hereford and Aberdeen Angus, preferably bulls, but sometimes also cows, that are thirty months old because, according to Jody Storch, they have a more complex flavor.

Competitors

Despite its success Luger has never considered moving to Manhattan. Former colleagues have been trying to open their own chic versions of the Luger style steakhouse since the middle of the 80s with a similar minimal menu and the same superior ripened steaks. The result is a list of very successful devotees in New York, which has made it the steak capital of the world. They owe their success to the bankers, Wall Street brokers and other white-collar workers who have made these no-nonsense steakhouses their favorite hangouts. Prices have also increased as a result and at the end of the day you pay similar prices to what you would expect at a European three-star restaurant. The Forman heirs keep a good eye out for the competition, but even after 100 years they have not seen a reduction in their clientele. They were even awarded their first Michelin star in 2010, to their own amazement.

PETER LUGER STEAKHOUSE,
178 BROADWAY,
BROOKLYN, NEW YORK

One of the oldest and most famous brasseries in Paris is Le Relais de Venise. They are world-famous for their sirloin steak with green butter-tarragon sauce, and as can be expected the recipe has been a family secret since 1959.

'Cette Entrecôte n'a aucune succersale dans Paris'. This is printed in gold letters on the glass door of the Le Relais de Venise l'Entrecôte restaurant, which is its name in full. Roughly translated the sentence means: this restaurant has no other branches in Paris. The reason for this is that there were quite a few imitations of the famous Paris brasserie that wanted to share in the success of 'L'Entrecôte', as it is known in Paris.

Every day during lunchtime and in the evenings people stand in long lines, waiting to be seated, including the usual tourists from America and Japan, but also a considerable amount of French-speaking people. Once guests leave the restaurant the hostess, a French lady with a coquettish bun of bleached-blond hair and an icy smile, invites a new group of waiting customers to come inside -'*Vite, vite s'il vous plaît!*' Once inside the brasserie, spread over two floors, you notice that all of the small tables are occupied. Of all the many Parisian brasseries that serve steak frites, Le Relais de Venise – located near Porte Maillot, a ten minute walk west of the Arc de Triomphe – is one of the most famous. The brasserie has become famous due to its cast iron formula: there is no menu available (only a dessert menu). For over half a century the brasserie has only served steak frites.

Since 1959

The history of the restaurant dates back to 1959 when founder Paul Gineste de Saurs took over the Italian restaurant Le Relais de Venise in Paris. He swapped the Italian menu for a menu with only steak frites and a wine list with wines from its own wine chateau: Château de Saurs in Toulouse. Instead of the usual herb butter they also served steak with green butter-tarragon sauce, which quickly became famous in Parisian circles.

After the death of the founder his heirs continued with the successful formula under various names.

Daughter Hélène also founded establishments in locations such as London and New York by licensing partners that bear the same name. Son Henri opened a chain with an identical formula in French cities such as Bordeaux, Toulouse and Lyon under the name L'Entrecôte. Another daughter, Marie-Paule, started various businesses in Paris and in the middle east under a different name – Le Relais de l'Entrecôte.

Lacquered heels

The interior of Le Relais de Venise is as you would expect from a traditional French bistro: wooden brasserie chairs, brass ornaments, red curtains, wooden panels and tables covered with white paper. The waiters – exclusively female – are dressed in black dresses with white lace trim, traditional white pinafores and black lacquered heels. They deftly maneuver large heated trays as they serve steak frites at the packed, noisy tables. The choice is clear: do we want ours '*bleu*', '*saignant*', '*à point*' or '*bien cuit*'? The order is written in code on the paper tablecloth: '2 x AP' (*à point*). The appetizer, which is a part of the standard menu, is placed on the table within five minutes without us having asked for it and with no explanation given: a simple but tasty green salad with a mustard vinaigrette and crumbled walnut. The house wine is a bottle from the family's own vineyards.

The sirloin is precut – in two portions – and served from trays, which are kept warm on a hot plate, topped with the famous green butter-tarragon sauce. There has been much speculation about the sauce. An investigative journalist from Le Monde, a French daily newspaper, smuggled some of the sauce out of the restaurant and had it analyzed in a laboratory. He wrote that the source is based on a few ingredients, including chicken livers. The heirs of Saurs immediately denied this with great firmness. The ingredients that can be readily identified include parsley, shallots, mustard, lemon and white wine.

Secret

The sauce tastes good, the steak is nicely cooked, exactly as we wanted it. We had a few reservations about the meat, however, as it did not have a nice rim of fat. It seemed to be an ordinary piece of knuckle, rather than a sirloin steak. Not that there is anything wrong with that, it just needs to be pointed out that this is not a sirloin steak. The dessert menu that follows consists of fine brasserie classics such as profiteroles, tarte tatin and crème caramel. This was washed down with an espresso and, after exactly 45 minutes, along came the bill. A modest Euro 64 (including Euro 14 for the wine) for two people, without coffee.

When we asked Madame Lucienne, who appeared to be the hostess, if we could have a look around in the kitchen to see how the steaks are made, we were met with a very firm 'non'. She then opened the door to let us out with the same icy smile, before inviting the next guests with the familiar '*Vite, vite s'il vous plaît!*'

LE RELAIS DE VENICE,
271 BOULEVARD PEREIRE, PARIS
WWW.RELAISDEVENISE.COM

Belgium has always been a mecca for lovers of a perfect steak. Every village and every town has at least one or more brasseries that serve superior steak frites. But there is one dish that most Belgians, Walloons and Flemings, have enjoyed for many years now: the côte à l'os from Christophe and Anne Duthoit at Saint-Cornil restaurant in Aalbeke (in the Kortrijk region) in the northern Belgian province of West Flanders. The location also makes it the ideal lunch stop for anyone on the way to the Netherlands or to Paris.

Simply leave the highway at Kortrijk and 10 minutes later you enter the sleepy village of Aalbeke. Located on the square, next to the church and opposite the local liquor store, is the family restaurant cum butchery Saint Cornil. This is an ordinary eatery in the finest Belgian tradition, which has nothing to do with Michelin stars. This restaurant, with 150 seats, is nevertheless nearly always completely full, from Monday to Friday and not just in the evenings; even during lunchtime it is difficult to find a free table. The specialty of the house: côté à l'os (also called côte de boeuf), which has been served in the same way since 1965 with either a homemade piccalilli sauce and/or Béarnaise.

When you enter Saint Cornil you noticed that the decor is based on the cozy 50s, with lots of neatly polished brass ornaments, burgundy tablecloths and dark brown wood paneling. There are dozens of statues of cows and bulls of all sorts, sizes, colors and materials on the bar, on the fireplace and in cabinets. The charm of Saint Cornil is that all guests have received the same menu for almost half a century. For the all-inclusive rate of Euro 38 you get: the aperitif of the house, an appetizer of your choice (home-made pâté, fillet with an egg or *beenhesp*, which is Flemish for roast ham), and a main course with côte de boeuf (alternatively: rib of lamb or leg of lamb), with a side of fries and lettuce and one dessert of Irish Coffee or ice cream, as you prefer. Half a bottle of wine or a pint of Belgian beer is also included in the price.

Belgian Blue

Christophe, the owner of the restaurant, prepares the meat every day with his own hands on 'the stove', which is located in the middle of the restaurant. He uses a red-hot (gas) grill with a lava stone on which he grills the meat on the bone. He works with the Belgian Blue, which is the most popular meat cattle in Belgium. Christophe: "I'm doing this because my father used to do it, which is typical for Belgians." His meat comes from his own butchery, which is located right next to the restaurant, which is where his father started his own butchery in the late 50s. He then decided to also open a cafe next to the butchery. The people who visited his cafe often wanted to have something to eat before they went home and not long afterwards the steaks of Duthoit became a household name. The meat, which comes from suppliers in the area, is personally selected by Christophe. "It is a matter of feeling – the meat must be nice and red, not too light and not too dark, and it must have a good layer of fat." They do not receive any portioned steaks here that are carefully vacuum-packed, which is the norm at many other restaurants. Christophe and his son Jean François receive the entire back of an animal, which they then bone by hand in the butchery to obtain perfect pieces of côté à l'os.

Legendary piccalilli sauce

"I always grill our côté à l'os saignant," said Christophe above his grill. With a practiced movement he punctured the meat with a large meat fork to turn it around. One côté à l'os for two people weighs more than 2 pounds, including the bone. First of all he browns the meat all around over a low temperature on a griddle. How long? "Every piece of meat is different, but I think 15 minutes is a good average." The côté à l'os is then put on the glowing hot gas grill with a lava stone for another five minutes where the meat is further grilled with a loud hiss. Only at the end does he add coarsely ground pepper and salt. The finishing touch is a dash of brandy, which briefly engulfs the steak in high flames to provide a bit of extra grilled flavor.
The steaks are then cut into slices of about one

inch with a sharp carving knife and served around the bone on wooden boards. The side dishes consist of crispy fries and fresh lettuce (with an egg and a slice of tomato on top), which are served in retro style on aluminum containers which Van der Valk has always held the patent for. Delicious with pickled cucumbers, onions and peppers that are placed all over the table. The legendary home-made piccalilli sauce and tangy Béarnaise go very well with the perfect côté à l'os from Christophe.

RESTAURANT SAINT-CORNIL,
AALBEKEPLAATS 15
AALBEKE, BELGIUM

STEAK

FROM FIELD TO TABLE

Addresses, index and acknowledgements

Butchers

Wagyu
WWW.WAGYUSHOP.NL
Private individuals can also order Wagyu meat from De Drie Morgen farm in the Netherlands, which stocks only 100% pure Wagyu.

YOLANDA AND FRED DE LEEUW
The most famous butchery in Amsterdam. One of the few Dutch butcheries where Wagyu beef can be bought. They also stock a few other exclusive types of cattle, such as the very tasty Rubia from Spain.
YOLANDA AND FRED DE LEEUW BUTCHERY
UTRECHTSESTRAAT 92
AMSTERDAM, THE NETHERLANDS
WWW.SLAGERIJDELEEUW.NL

Dry-aged meat
WWW.DRYAGEDVLEES.NL
Top quality dry-aged meat delivered at home in the Netherlands via the website of the Chateaubriand butchery, packed in a styrofoam box with added refrigeration to ensure that the meat arrives in an excellent condition. Ordered today, delivered tomorrow, seven days a week.

CHATEAUBRIAND
This much-lauded eatery/butchery in Heemstede, in the Netherlands specializes in dry-aged meat from Scottish Aberdeen Angus cattle.
Aged in their own dry-aged cell. Unrivaled quality côte de boeuf, rib-eye and sirloin, but lesser-known cuts can also be bought on location.
CHATEAUBRIAND,
BINNENWEG 163, HEEMSTEDE, THE NETHERLANDS
WWW.CHATEAUBRIAND.NL

USA Beef
WWW.BEEFENSTEAK.NL
This Dutch online butchery sells a very fine selection of foreign beef, including beef from America (grain-fed beef), South America and Belgium (the famous Belgian dikbillen).

VLOT BUTCHERY VOF
This independent village butchery in the village of Brandwijk in the Netherlands only sells meat from animals slaughtered by the butcher himself. Anyone looking for an exotic cut of meat in the Netherlands can get in touch with Bert Vlot's butchery, which is only open on Thursdays, Fridays and Saturdays. It is well worth the trip.
VLOT BUTCHERY VOF
DAMSEWEG 68, BRANDWIJK, THE NETHERLANDS (NO WEBSITE)

OTTOMANELLI BROTHERS
This Italian butchery in Upper East Side in New York has more than 100 years of tradition, with sawdust on the floor, black-and-white family photos on the wall and a display of fantastic, quality American steaks. Specialty: USDA Prime Beef, matured in-house for at least three weeks.
OTTOMANELLI BROS
1549 YORK AVENUE
NEW YORK, WWW.NYCOTTO.COM

THE MEAT HOOK
It seems to be very hip to become a butcher in New York City. Just ask the latest generation of butchers in The Meat Hook in Brooklyn. They enjoy 'butchering' to lounge music in the cooking school, cookbook shop and lunchroom. With fantastic home-made burgers and sausages made from 100% sustainable meat from EcoFarm.
THE MEAT HOOK,
100 FROST STREET, BROOKLYN
NEW YORK, WWW.THEBROOKLYNKITCHEN.COM

Restaurants

The Netherlands

MIDTOWN GRILL

A New York style steakhouse, located next to the Marriott Hotel (near the Leidseplein). Here you do not eat steak, but Creekstone Farm USDA Prime corn-fed Black Angus Beef. Juicy dry-aged steaks, imported directly from the United States of America. Choose your favorite steak from the trolley that the waiter rolls to your table.

MIDTOWN GRILL,
STADHOUDERSKADE 12
AMSTERDAM
WWW.MIDTOWNGRILL.NL

POMPSTATION

This is a wonderful place, located on the site of a former gas station from 1912, with a remarkably wide selection of steaks, e.g. from Dutch MRY cattle, Beemsterland, dry-aged American Angus sirloin and even Wagyu beef. Served with Luie wijven frites (in-house name for fries) and homemade mayonnaise.

POMPSTATION BAR & GRILL,
ZEEBURGERDIJK 52, AMSTERDAM
WWW.POMPSTATION.NU

LOETJE

From a simple Amsterdam neighborhood cafe with billiard tables to a chain with several locations (Amsterdam, Laren, Ouderkerk a/d Amstel and Overveen, all in the Netherlands). Here you can enjoy – at a modest price of € 15.95 – an acceptable fillet steak, swimming in gravy, with white bread, fries and a bowl of lettuce.

CAFÉ LOETJE,
JOHANNES VERMEERSTRAAT 52,
AMSTERDAM
WWW.CAFELOETJE.NL (MULTIPLE LOCATIONS)

THE HARBOUR CLUB

Dry-aged Black Angus NY strip steak or côte de boeuf from Piet van de Berg's MRY beef with thick fries and homemade mayonnaise. If that is not to your liking you can also get chateaubriand or escalope in this classy eatery located in the city park under the Euromast in Rotterdam (with a second establishment in the Scheveningen harbor) in the Netherlands.

THE HARBOUR CLUB ROTTERDAM
KIEVITSLAAN 25, ROTTERDAM
THE HARBOUR CLUB SCHEVENINGEN
DR. LELYKADE 5-13
SCHEVENINGEN
WWW.THEHARBOURCLUB.NL

L'ENTRECÔTE ET LES DAMES

A clever copy of the famous French brasserie chain L'Entrecôte, by the ladies from the more distant Brasserie of Baerle in Amsterdam. The formula is tried and tested: salad (with mustard mayo), sirloin steak and French fries for € 23.50. Fine sirloin from Dutch Meuse-Rhine-Yssel sirloin beef with a homemade garlic butter sauce. Those who prefer something other than meat can also enjoy sole, baked in cream butter and served with Ravigotte sauce.

L' ENTRECÔTE ET LES DAMES,
VAN BAERLESTRAAT 47–49
AMSTERDAM
WWW.ENTRECOTE-ET-LES-DAMES.NL

CAFÉ GEORGES

French brasserie in New York style in the heart of Amsterdam. Always crowded and boisterous. White tiles and waiters donned in white. Iconic steaks and fries like those you would eat in Paris and New York. Also open for breakfast and lunch.

LEIDSEGRACHT 84, WILLEMSPARKWEG 74
AND UTRECHTSESTRAAT 17
AMSTERDAM
WWW.CAFEGEORGE.NL

Restaurants

New York
WOLFGANG'S STEAKHOUSE
Modern classic, high-end, NY-style steakhouse, owned by Wolfgang Zwiener, former head waiter at Peter Luger, who worked there for forty years before he started his own place. Favored by Wall Street brokers and bankers. Various branches in New York, with the flagship restaurant on Park Avenue.
4 PARK AVENUE/409
GREENWICH STREET/200 EAST 54TH STREET,
WWW.WOLFGANGSSTEAKHOUSE.NET

PETER LUGER
Now in the hands of the third generation descendants of the late Sol Forman, who took over the hundred year old restaurant in Brooklyn in the 50s and converted it into the most famous steakhouse in the city. This old school NY steakhouse serves Porterhouse that is dry-aged in-house, hissing as it is served on a plate, swimming in butter. Popular with tourists and locals.
178 BROADWAY,
BROOKLYN, NEW YORK
WWW.PETERLUGER.COM

THE OLD HOMESTEAD
Located in downtown Manhattan in the Meat Packing District, where all the butchers used to be in days gone by. "We're the king of beef" it says on a life-sized cow on the facade. And that is exactly what The Old Homestead stands for: NY steaks of the best quality. The oldest steakhouse in New York, since 1886.
56 9TH AVENUE, NEW YORK
WWW.THEOLDHOMESTEADSTEAKHOUSE.COM

Paris
Paris naturally has too many brasseries to discuss them all here. We will limit ourselves to two, including a real insider tip (courtesy of Leon Mazairac).

LE BISTROT DU PEINTRE
Here you can get côte de boeuf (20 ounces) or sirloin steak (13 ounces) until 2 o'clock in the morning. Parisian chefs also enjoy coming here after work to enjoy a genuine French steak.
LE BISTROT DU PEINTRE,
116 AVENUE LEDRU ROLLIN,
PARIS, FRANCE
WWW.BISTROTDUPEINTRE.COM

LE RELAIS DE VENISE L'ENTRECÔTE
One of the oldest and most famous brasseries in Paris is located close to the Porte Maillot station and it owes its slightly overrated reputation to its sirloin served with green butter-tarragon sauce. Long lines stand outside the door every day. With branches in New York and London.
LE RELAIS DE VENISE L'ENTRECÔTE
271 BOULEVARD PEREIRE
PARIS, FRANCE
WWW.RELAISDEVENISE.COM

Belgium

AU VIEUX PORT, ANTWERP

The côte de boeuf is rolled on a trolley to your table where it is cut. Delicious Béarnaise and divine fries make Vieux Port a top venue in the old port of Antwerp.

AU VIEUX PORT, NAPELSSTRAAT 130, ANTWERP, WWW.AUVIEUXPORT.BE

SAINT-CORNIL AALBEKE (KORTRIJK)

This has been a landmark in meat-loving Belgium for the past 35 years now. Côte de boeuf from Belgian dikbillen, from the adjacent butchery of the same owners. Well matured and seasoned to perfection. Served with pickles, homemade piccalilli and crispy fries.

SAINT-CORNIL, AALBEKEPLAATS 15, AALBEKE, TEL: +32 (0)56 41 35 23 (WWW.ST-CORNIL-AALBEKE.BE)

LA PAIX, ANDERLECHT (BRUSSELS)

This brasserie is more than 100 years old and currently former star chef David Martin holds sway here. Located opposite the slaughterhouse of Anderlecht. Eat in style. Côte de boeuf from Simmenthal beef or crispy confit Wagyu beef.

LA PAIX, ROPSY-CHAUDRONSTRAAT 49, BRUSSELS, WWW.LAPAIX1892.COM

LA TABLE DU BOUCHER, BERGEN (MONS)

Chef and butcher Luc Broutard selects the meat in the slaughterhouse. In his super cozy, no-nonsense brasserie in the heart of Bergen he only offers premium quality. He does not only serve super steak with fries, but just about any cut of beef, pork, veal and lamb.

LA TABLE DU BOUCHER, RUE D'HAVRÉ 49, BERGEN, WWW.LUCBROUTARD.BE

Kitchen equipment

Most of the equipment as shown in Tools & Techniques can be bought at specialty cooking stores and at better department stores. For a list of addresses of these shops (and their e-shops) see www.deperfectesteak.nl.

The products depicted in this book (p. 74 and 75) include:
Frying pans: De Buyer (steel),
Fissler (stainless steel), Mauviel (copper)
Knives: Laguiole and Aubrac
Roasting pan: Mauviel
Cutting board and wooden spatulas: Epicurean
Probe: CDN
Barbecue: Weber

(Thanks to Kookpunt Rotterdam for supplying the material required for the photographs)

While working as a food critic while writing this book during the past year and a few years prior to that I spoke to dozens of experts about the ins and outs of the perfect steak, including chefs, butchers, farmers, nutritionists and other food and drink connoisseurs. Thank you all for being so generous with your phenomenal knowledge and tips!

Rob Baars, Arthur Bremmer, Jonnie Boer, Rudolph Bos, Johannes van Dam, David Ciancio, Simon Dowling, Christophe en Ann Duthoit, Jan Groenewold, Jan Faber, Harold Hamersma, Cees Helder, Sergio Herman, Dirk Huisman, Freek Kamphuis, Jaap Klinkhamer, Ton van der Kolk, Eke Mariën, Leon Mazairac, William McLaren jr., Arno Mos, Nick Ottomanelli, Sander de Ponti, Boudewijn Roemers, Adele Teekens, Eymert Teekens, Bert Vlot, Kees Vlot, Arno Veenhof, Ria Schipper, Huub Schoemaker, Pepijn Schut, Felix Wilbrink, Arjen Zeevenhoven and anyone else I may have forgotten.

SPECIAL THANKS

Johan van Uden, manager of Chateaubriand butchery in Heemstede and two-time winner of the Golden Butcher's Ring, for his tireless explanations and enthusiasm about everything that has to do with the real butcher's trade.

COLOPHON

IDEA & TEXT: Marcus Polman/Nieuwe Haring Media
ART DIRECTION: Durk Hattink/Durk.com
PHOTOGRAPHY: Saskia van Osnabrugge,
except pp. 32/33: CRV/Veeteelt
IMAGE EDITING: Lisette Hesselink
STYLING: Jan-Willem van Riel/De Stijlbrouwerij
FOOD STYLING: Sander de Ponti
TECHNICAL ADVISOR: Johan van Uden/Chateaubriand
EDITORS: Ingrid van Koppenhagen
& Richard Heeres/Teksttalenten
PROJECT LEADER: Inge Huijs
PUBLISHER: Martin Fontijn/Fontaine Uitgevers

BOOKS

In writing this book I used the following reference and culinary books:
J.W. BARETTA (CHIEF EDITOR),
Handboek voor de slager, 1950
JAMES BEARD, American Cookery, 1972
HESTON BLUMENTHAL, In Search of Total Perfection, 2009
JOHANNES VAN DAM, Dedikkevandam, 2005
ALAN DAVIDSON, The Oxford Companion to Food, 2006
EKE MARIËN & JAN GROENEWOLD, Cook & Chemist, 2007
HAROLD MCGEE, Over eten en drinken, 2006
HAROLD MCGEE,
Goed koken, En wat je daarvoor moet weten, 2010
MICHAEL POLLAN, The Omnivore's Dilemma, 2008
MICHAEL POLLAN, Een pleidooi voor echt eten, 2010
JONATHAN SAFRAN FOER, Dieren eten, 2010
EDITORS OF COOK'S ILLUSTRATED MAGAZINE,
Steaks, Chops, Roasts and Ribs, 2004

Steak: From Field to Table
Text © 2011 by Marcus Polman/Fontaine Uitgevers
Photography © 2011 by Saskia van Osnabrugge/Fontaine Uitgevers

The information in this book was originally published in the following title:
Handboek Voor De Perfecte Steak
Text © 2011 by Marcus Polman/Fontaine Uitgevers
Photography © 2011 by Saskia van Osnabrugge/Fontaine Uitgevers
Originally published by Fontaine Uitgevers in the Netherlands

Translated by Network Languages, Ltd.

First published in the United States of America in 2013 by Betterway Home Books, an imprint of F+W Media, Inc., 10151 Carver Rd., Suite 200, Blue Ash Ohio, 45242 (800) 289-0963. First Edition.

www.fwmedia.com

ISBN-13: 978-1-4403-3161-9

17 16 15 14 13   5 4 3 2 1